How To Run A Successful Real Estate Business

Insider Tips for Real Estate Agents on How to Work Less and Earn More

JEN DUMITRESCU

Efficiency is what will ensure that you stand out in the future and build a company that will help you retire and lead the next best life.

—*Jen Dumitrescu*

TABLE OF CONTENTS

Foreword   vii

A Little About Me   1
Intro   3
Where to Start   5
Picking a Brokerage   7
Google Your Name   12
Branding   15
Marketing   19
Social Media   32
Business Plans   37
Website   42
Systemizing Your Business   50
Delegation   55
Databases   65
Accounting   68
Tools to Organize Your [Work] Life   82
How to Get New Clients   91
Coaching   96
Conferences   101
Staging   103
Insurance   106
Building a Good Network of Service Providers   111
Maintaining Your Health and Sanity   113
Be Professional   119
Reading List   121
Thank You   123

FOREWORD

I know what you're thinking: Why is a consultant who works with organizations on improving their sales experience writing a forward for a book about real estate?

I met Jen over 18 years ago when we were both working at the same Toronto-based software company. She was in marketing, I was in sales, and we both worked for bosses that drove us to drink. Our stints at that company were short-lived but our friendship has endured; proof that something awesome can blossom from a quagmire of mediocrity.

Throughout the years, we both have applied our unique set of skills in marketing and sales to our careers; until we both decided it was time to build a career for ourselves. In my case, I started up a consultancy focused on guiding SaaS businesses on how they can improve their sales effectiveness through the sales experience. In Jen's case, she started up her career in real estate. How we approached these two vastly different industries was with one common thread: The experience that people have with us needs to be memorable, valuable and unique.

Ultimately, people buy because of the experience they have with you. Whether you are selling clothing, software, or homes… the experience can either make or break the sale. Think about the last large purchase you made. How much of your decision to buy was guided by the salesperson? Did you make the purchase because of, or in spite of, that salesperson? Would you buy from them again?

How Jen and I have structured our businesses is directly correlated to the experiences that we have had, and have provided, over our careers. And now, those experiences have been charted out so that you can benefit from what Jen has learned works – and doesn't work! – when trying to build out a career in real estate. Instead of trying to figure it all out for yourself, Jen has laid it all out for you, so you can focus on providing your unique value and an amazing sales experience to your potential clients.

I've experienced the techniques Jen discusses in this book first-hand – not as her friend, but as her client – as she guided my husband and me through the purchase of our first home. An experience that for some folks would have destroyed a years-long friendship; but for us, solidified a friendship that will last a lifetime.

I hope you enjoy this book as much as I have enjoyed watching Jen apply the techniques in it to make her career a success.

T. Melissa Madian, P.Eng.
Founder & Chief Fabulous Officer
TMM Enablement Services, Inc.
Author of: *Enabler? I Hardly Know Her! How to Make the Sales Experience Not Suck*
Toronto, Canada – August 2020

Thanks!

I am lucky to have really wonderful people in my life. People who make me laugh, encourage me to try new things, and to be brave. Some of them see the world with plenty of colours, some in black-and-white. Both are so important because they add different perspectives to life. **Thank you to all _you_ wonderful people.**

I'm thankful for my clients. I've have learned so much about myself, about people, about relationships. During my time working with clients, I've laughed so hard I've had tears run down my face, I've cried alongside them during their difficult situations, and I've almost thrown up in some really dirty homes. Most importantly I've learned that real estate is not a job; it's a passion.

A LITTLE BIT ABOUT ME

First and foremost, my goal with this book is to help you. If you would like to know a bit more about me and how I came up with the idea of this book, it is outlined below. If you would like to skip right to the content, I'm totally fine with that too.

My sales career started with a red wagon and boxes of Girl Guide cookies at the age of six. I had big dreams of being the 'area' superstar. From there, it just kept escalating: various retail jobs, some exciting: GAPKIDS, some not so much—selling stemware and bad home decor items that made me cringe (and I was fifteen at the time) to working at large corporations like Rogers and Scotiabank. Most of my career has been in sales jobs minus one BAD episode of working as a renewal manager at a domain name registration company job (it only took me seven months to learn that as a salesperson I MUCH preferred doing and getting things done versus having to write proposals as to WHY I wanted to do something). My other oddball, completely unrelated job was as an ISO 9000 quality control coordinator, where I was writing processes for how companies operated.

All of my sales jobs were at companies that offered extensive training: courses like Seven Habits of Highly Effective People (Stephen R. Covey), management training, various personality training courses, and negotiation courses. I always said that after university, I would never go back to school, and yet, at every job, I took EVERY single course being offered by the company. It turns out that I never did want to stop learning—I just had to learn things that were of interest to me.

Who knew that the ISO 9000 job, where I was systematizing and creating processes for every possible action at a company, would be my dark horse. Once I got into real estate, I realized that the only way to grow, be efficient, and not go crazy was to have systems and processes. And here we are: I've taken twenty-seven years (or thirty-eight years if you want to count my cookie-slinging days) of learning processes and fifteen years of real estate in an extremely competitive market and created what will hopefully streamline your business, give you more free time, and keep you doing what you love best.

INTRO

What they don't tell you when you are studying to become a real estate agent (in Ontario specifically) is that the courses are designed to give you the basics in handling a real estate transaction only. What it doesn't teach you is that you are going to be running a business. So, anyone looking to run a BUSINESS versus just having a career will need help.

One of the very first books I read, when I got into real estate was *The E-Myth Revisited: Why Most Small Businesses Don't Work and What to Do About It* by Michael E Gerber. I've always known that in order for real estate to be more than just a career, I would need to build something that was sellable business in the future. In order to do that, I knew I would have to

   a) Be aware of all the various elements of running a business,
   b) Systemize my business so that only the really critical elements required my attention, and
   c) Make sure I was running every area as efficiently as possible.

It's important to look at the big picture—the big BUSINESS picture. Lots of mistakes can be made, or lots of money can be wasted, if you don't look at the big picture. I wish someone had shared all these insights with me when I started out. Which is why I wanted to share them with you.

Hopefully, this book can save you a lot of time, aggravation, and mistakes and keep you moving forward at all times.

The design of this book is meant to make the various steps easy and POSSIBLE for you to accomplish. I have not filled the pages with lots of extra fluff as to why I did things one way or the other. This is because I hate reading unnecessary fluff and, let's face it—building your business systems and creating some automation is a VERY large task, and just doing that stuff will take more than enough time. There's no point in having to read a really long book on top of it.

It's time to get down to business.

WHERE TO START

This book is meant for both the new agent and the experienced agent.

To some degree, it can be a little bit like a "Choose Your Own Adventure™" book.

If you are a newly licensed agent, just reading this book is a step in the right direction. Some other areas you might want to focus on first:

Creating a productive website—that doesn't break the bank.
Determining your list of potential clients.
Developing a plan for your year (both a marketing and business plan).

If you are more experienced, you probably have some of the basics down. Topics that might be of more interest to you are:

Systemizing your business
Databases
Delegation
Tools to organize your life
Accounting

OR if you are looking to do a complete overhaul of your whole business: start at the beginning.

Regardless of whether you are new or an experienced agent, you will find a few of the topics are intertwined: that is, marketing with branding, branding with URL availability, etc.

If you have the time, read through it once and then circle back to see the best areas to start for your business.

I've included "Pro-Tips" throughout. These are things that I have learned that can really save time, money, or are just good to know (in my opinion).

PICKING A BROKERAGE (WHAT NO ONE TELLS YOU WHEN YOU BEGIN THIS JOURNEY)

This section can be relevant if you are BRAND new to real estate or if you are thinking about making a brokerage change OR if you hadn't considered it—and maybe should be considering it.

Before I worked in real estate, I was an "employee." I worked for various companies; I got the jobs by interviewing for them. The process was very much about us determining if we would be a good fit for each other.

Me: Did I like the job description? The manager I would report to? Did I see potential in the company growth-wise?

Them: Did they feel I was the right candidate for the job? Would I be a good team player? Or fit the company culture.

Real estate (for the most part) has a COMPLETELY different model.

YOU pay the brokerage to work there. While there may be a small percentage of instances where what I am about to write is not the case, this is largely the model I've seen in Toronto with many of the big offices. Most brokerages want you to sign up at their office because they make money from you being there. In addition to collecting some of your commission, some also charge a monthly fee or a per-transaction fee. If you have a real estate license, seem capable, and have had no major run-ins with the law—why wouldn't they want you to work with them? I'm simplifying it a bit, but that's the model generally.

What I didn't know getting into real estate was what a KEENER I must have looked like, coming from my corporate interviewing background. I met with a few managers; I asked them questions about culture, and how they would support me. I listened to them mostly talk about why their office was the best, why having "their brand" associated with my name would make or break my business, and how their brand was what the consumer recognized, and THAT would be why they wanted to work with me. Being new to self-employment, I was scared. Surely being with the BIG Brand Named office would help me?

This is my opinion: the real estate office model in many, many cities, towns, provinces is largely broken. It's based on the brokerage, saying, "We are the best because," and "Yup we have some training manuals you can read," and "What can you do for us and why we are the best."

What I learned (and what they don't tell you)
The public is generally very uneducated about real estate offices. Nine times out of ten, my friends and family had NO IDEA where I worked. They often confused the company I worked for with our biggest competitor. Which says a few things to me:

- Real estate companies are not doing enough to distinguish themselves in the marketplace.
- There is a general lack of education in the marketplace (which is fine; it's not our client's job to know the various companies) and it doesn't matter. Of course, sometimes, you will meet someone whose perception is that "company X" can do a better job. If you are working for one of the "big guys," everything just blurs together. If you happen to work for a brokerage that is paving a new path, being supportive to its agents, and having a client focus, congratulations!

Here are some of my key findings from working at one of the "big" companies:

Zero support: If you are new to real estate, find an office that can support new agents. There are so many "real" things to learn that are not taught in the courses and so many questions. If you don't have a manager who can be there to answer your questions (and sometimes at night), it can be very difficult, scary, and lonely. It can be very much a sink-or-swim model.

About four years into the business, I moved to a different brokerage. This was a large office with a lot of top performing agents. I remember, on more than one occasion, needing to speak with a manager and never hearing back. It would often take many calls, emails, or messages left with the office for me to receive a call back. Calling my manager was usually a last resort for me, so to be in a situation where I did really need guidance and not be able to receive it (regularly) was frustrating.

PRO-TIP: Ask to speak to a new-ish agent. Maybe someone who has been in the business for a year. Ask how they find the support. Is the training being offered even relevant? How are the manager call back times?

Marketing: Some offices consider themselves progressive because they have "templates" for some of the basics you need to get started. As I will explain below, generally, you are not the only person using this, and therefore you are at risk of looking just like everyone else. Not to mention, I've found that it's plain and outdated. Even if they have a marketing team to help you, ask to see some of the materials they have produced. I learned the hard way that the "marketing team" meant people who could design stuff in PowerPoint, only with very bad to horrible graphics, that made me cringe. And I was being charged for their time to do the work.

What is the brokerage's stance on an "informed" client?

There is a lot of controversy in the media about real estate agents and how much information we share with clients. As well as about how much information SHOULD be shared with clients. Depending on your stance, it might be helpful to work at a brokerage that shares the same philosophy as you.

For example, if you believe the real estate market should be more transparent in its dealings and your office does not share that same belief, you might find your opportunities to conduct business in a manner that is comfortable for you hindered.

What is the office atmosphere? Is it an environment that promotes idea sharing?

Real estate can be very lonely and isolating. It's easy to get caught up in your own head. It's nice to be in an office environment where everyone shares and genuinely wants to help. If you have questions, would you have a reliable network of agents to call or pick their brain?

Manager: Even experienced agents need great brokers. There are always new issues, questions, and situations for which you will be turning to your broker for advice. Can you trust them? Are they available to help? Are they reputable in the industry? (This can mean more than you know should there ever be a major issue.) Are they patient? Will they have your back in a conflict situation? What is their conflict resolution manner?

Spend some time with them. Are they easy to talk to? Your manager can be vital in building your reputation as a well-respected ethical agent.

Finally, if you have worked at an office, working at a real estate office can be completely different from a respect perspective. I've never seen a work environment where so many people feel entitled to treat other people poorly. Obviously, that's not the case for everyone. However, it does happen. Agents treat admin staff poorly, or even other agents. For the most part, since everyone is self-employed, it's sometimes tolerated. Of course, this is no reason to be rude to any other colleague or fellow staff member, but it happens. In one office that I worked at, the higher producing agents would regularly swear or yell at the manager or admin staff. Because many offices are earning money from agents to work there, they tolerate this kind of behaviour. It's quite twisted. Be aware of the office environment. Is it aligned with who you are as a person?

The biggest lesson I learned was that I was scared. I had no idea what to expect from working for myself, and again, coming from a corporate world, this was way different, and I BELIEVED the real estate company I was working for would have my back. The reality was that minus a handful of people who are still in my life, I was just a number. To some degree, some offices sell fear. It's hard not to buy it when you don't know any better and are starting out. My current office has a very different attitude and cares for its agents. Having been at various offices, I can clearly identify the difference. It's big, it's an enormous difference.

GOOGLE YOUR NAME

Whether you are starting your business or rebranding, before you go down the long road of picking a business name or deciding on a dream URL for yourself, Google your name to see what comes up. This will help guide you as to what options might be possible from a business name/branding perspective. For example, is there someone else with your chosen name? Another style of business with a similar name? Does a porn star show up as the first hit? (Don't laugh; it actually happens) Are there photos that show up that you don't want? Any negative articles or statements? It's best to know what your customers might stumble on if they do the same.

Email:
For most people, getting an email address is the quickest way to legitimize your business and start DOING something work-related. I'm sure you already have one, which is great to get started with until you have finished reading the next few chapters.

Your email address should match your website URL for consistency, user-friendliness, and clear marketing.

The section on websites explains about picking a URL. Having an email and URL that match is best for consistency. But it's not always possible. Be mindful. Having a URL of "sellhomeswithX" and then an email address which is X@myhomesX.com could be confusing.

PRO-TIP: It's up to you if you would like to jump forward to the BRANDING AND MARKETING section of the book, as it will come into play for picking your URL. Or maybe just read both sections, so you are well covered.

For emails, it's best to stick with something neutral—that is either your name or your tag line. What you want to avoid in this real estate life is having to change your email address numerous times.

Using one associated with your brokerage or your internet provider will result in this.

Example:

Jen@rogers.com

Jen@bell.ca

Jen@Xrealty.com

Jen@gmail.com

If you use something neutral and non-company dependent, you can move across the country and change internet companies, and no one will be the wiser. It also saves having to send out that, "Oh, hey, my email has now changed to X," too many times.

Example:

jen@jend.ca

Bob@bobrealestate.ca

It's also good to think about a scalable email, should you wish to have an assistant or a team working with you. Is the domain name flexible enough to still make sense when various people join? For example: Info@jend.ca or customerservice@jend.ca.

It's also important to think about length. Something that is too long increases the risk of typos. And, does anyone like typing a super long email address? NO!

Hosting/email platform:
As mentioned in the website section—where you host your website is key to your email address. Reliability is key. If your email address is associated with an internet provider and they are down (or broken), you are at risk for downtime and/or lost emails.

My email is hosted on a Google Business Platform that provides:

1. Amazing reliability
2. Increased storage (no need to worry about an oversized inbox)
3. Increased accessibility: the ability to access anywhere in the world on most devices
4. Ease of use: being able to connect your email and calendar seamlessly
5. Better security—no one wants a hacked account
6. Portability: no matter where your website is hosted, you have access to your email and no worries about moving your saved emails

BRANDING

A brand is something that distinctly identifies you (and your services) to your clients. It's something that states what you do—it's your reputation—and it distinguishes you from other people.

Branding can be in how your name/logo appears and also in the messaging you choose to use.

In today's market, a strong brand is important because consumers want a more personalized experience. So you need one!

And before you go about ordering a bunch of marketing material and creating your website, it's advisable to give this some thought.

This is also an opportunity to capitalize on the fact that many agents are not aware of this and have been doing their branding (i.e. doing it themselves and doing it physically) in such an old-school way that if done correctly, you can stand out.

Times have changed. Our clients (buyers and sellers) do still need help (despite all the information that is available to them online). They would like us to guide them and serve them. They want to be heard, and we need to make sure we are connecting and working with them in a way that THEY want.

Be you. Don't be who you think you are supposed to be. You will attract more people who you WANT to be working with because like attracts like. You can't be everything to everyone—by being you, you and your clients will have a much more enjoyable experience working together.

There are many different online and print resources to help guide you in creating your brand. Many companies can help you with this should you want. The advantage of using a company is that they will help guide you through the process of determining what an appropriate brand will be for you and ensure that the right message is being created and relayed.

It's also possible your brokerage has templates for you to use to get you started.

However, having worked with a few different brokerages, many times, these templates are quite dated. And very basic. So they might not resonate well with who you want your target market to be. Furthermore, the goal is to stand out, be different, not blend in with the crowd.

Your brand is what will be communicated through all the various marketing materials you use:

- Business cards
- Your website
- Your "For Sale" and "Open House" signs
- All print pieces
- Any other promotional materials that you use

If you work with a company to create your brand, chances are they will produce mock-ups of all these different elements so you can get a feel of how it will look in all the different scenarios.

Having the long last name that I do, I quickly realized that trying to have a brand that incorporates "Dumitrescu" would make it very difficult for any print piece to look good, and it just wouldn't on smaller print pieces. Not only that I also risked a higher rates of typos should clients or people who did not know me try entering it online or try to pronounce it. It's just awkward. And I prefer to make things easy for people.

The most common question to be answered when looking at developing a brand is: "Who is my target audience/market?" If you are new to real estate, this may not be very clear.

One suggestion for this might be to determine who you would like it to be and then create your brand around that. It's highly possible that over the years, you might revisit your brand and change it as your business grows. I personally have done it a few times. But it is important to have something when you start out.

One mistake many realtors make is trying to copy what someone else has done. I'll touch on this a bit more in the "marketing" section, but one thing I can say is that there is no benefit in being the same as someone else. And realtors are, for the most part, not designers or marketers, and as such many, MANY of the realtor brands are very confusing and not visually appealing. For this reason alone, it might be best to invest some money upfront to work with a company that will develop a professional, visually pleasing brand for you. It is, after all, your business.

Branding also ties heavily into your website. Many websites (realtor and non-realtor) are overloaded with information, which can be unappealing to consumers and can also leave them feeling confused. One company that I have learned a lot from and have adopted many of their philosophies is Storybrand by Donald Miller (www.storybrand.com). One of their key messages is—less is more and simplification. In a world where there are so many confusing messages, being clear can mean the difference between someone choosing to work with you or not. I find this particularly practical because it also means less work in creating content for your website that might not need to be there.

MARKETING

This is where so many agents get it wrong. REALLY wrong. Embarrassingly sometimes. For the most part, unless you have a background in marketing, graphic design, or design of some sort, this is an area better left to professionals. Or, perform your own research. Marketing techniques are always changing and will largely be dependent on your target market. A lot of marketing, especially if you are just starting out, will be trial and error. Be open to changing things up and being responsive to the marketplace in which you work.

PRO-TIP: Just because someone else is doing it doesn't mean it actually works. Test things for yourself to know for sure.

This topic can be broken down into a few categories:

1. How you should market YOURSELF
2. The marketing plan
3. How you should market your listings
4. The nitty-gritty of marketing materials

<u>Marketing yourself</u>
Developing your brand is the first step; however, some of the questions below will also come into play when trying to develop your brand as well as in trying to develop your marketing plan.

Here are some things to consider:

1. Who is your target audience? Think about who you are, what you offer, and who you are most likely to resonate/feel comfortable working with. How do people want to interact with you? What do you want them to see? What do you believe in? How do they like to be communicated with? What, about the home buying or selling process, can make them feel connected to you?

2. Who is your competition? How, in a sea of realtors and homes, can you distinguish yourself/your listing? How do you want to be different? What feels most comfortable for you?

3. Do you want a mission statement, sentence, and key phrase that describes what you plan to offer your clients?

    PRO-TIP: Instead of making it about how YOU are the best, consider what your market would like to hear. What would give them confidence in using you as their realtor? What are their fears/concerns? Consider using "you" versus "I" more often. Do make it something you believe in, though. Something demonstrable.

    Example 1: I'm the best realtor in the GTA because I win the most awards (BAD).

    Example 2: Real estate a different way. (Notice, I didn't use the word "I" there. Also, for the record, this is my tag line. I'm not saying it's the best, but it doesn't include the word I and I wasn't at risk of using some other realtor's tagline.)

PRO-TIP: Again, I highly encourage the Storybrand method (www.storybrand.com). Donald Miller's techniques are game-changers for both the self-employed person (from a business perspective) and the real estate market. His company does offer online courses (and in person, should you wish), which can help you create your brand/mission statement.

Our business model should be about making this experience for our customers, NOT US. Being aligned with that right out of the gate is going to mean the difference between being successful and UBER successful.

Mission statements give us a solid purpose in terms of what we are doing and allow us to structure all our business decisions through that filter. It allows us to be more streamlined in our activities because we know what we should be doing versus what we might want to do. A question to ask yourself when you are presented with a new idea is this: Is what you are doing in alignment with your mission statement? That is, if your mission statement is, "Helping seniors seamlessly transition from life home to their next home," and you aren't able to recommend a service provider for each possible step along the way, are you really helping them?

You may end up with various mission statements for:

- your business
- your buyers
- your sellers
- other people that you plan to interact with or help on this journey.

4. What is the best way to reach your target market? Print, online, social media? How about new potential clients versus your past clients? Is it best to use different mediums for each?

5. What's your budget? If you are unclear what something might cost do some research and then assign a value that you feel is fair. Modify throughout the year as necessary.

6. Monitor/track responses. This can be a bit harder to do with online/social media. If you do a mailing and can convert a client as a result of that particular mailing, you will have an idea of the return on investment (ROI). Social media is a harder ROI to measure. All marketing might take time … so be patient and consistent. Consistence can pay off. More on this very shortly.

Once you have reviewed the basics of your messaging and how you would like to differentiate yourself, it's wise to put it into a format that you can reference and work towards: The PLAN (or the marketing calendar as I often refer to it).

The importance of a marketing plan
You are running a business. All good (smart) businesses have a business plan and/or marketing plan. Having a plan will ensure that you are consistent with your efforts, your messages, and give you direction each month as to what should be happening. Furthermore, when you are self-employed, everything costs money. Having a marketing plan will make sure you are not just throwing money out the door.

Your plan might be divided up into a few categories:

1) Marketing to acquire new clients
2) Marketing for your listings
3) Marketing to your existing base.

Based on what you identified in answering the questions on the earlier pages, you should have some direction as to how you would like to build your marketing year. Keep in mind—if this is your first time doing it, by documenting it, you will be able to make adjustments in the following years as well as have a better idea of what works and the ROI from the various activities. If you fly by the seat of your pants, you will lose the ability to do this.

PRO-TIP: Use a year-long calendar; put all the different initiatives down on the left-hand side and plot out what will be done in each month. Print it and keep it in your office so you can see at a glance what is coming up and what needs to be done to prepare.

Some things to consider when planning out your calendar:

Mailed items, social media, online ads, promotions for open houses.

Communications with database (how many people you would like to call or communicate with monthly).

New business marketing plan (how to touch base with your farming market or new clients you are trying to reach).

Past client touchpoints (client parties, coffees, lunches, etc.).

Social media calendar.

Put together a budget of what this might cost you. Modify as necessary.

PRO-TIP: It's helpful to have a calendar planned out for the year with the major touchpoints. I've also found it beneficial to break it down into three-month intervals. You can be even more specific.

For example: Inspiration for new postcard mailers come to me at the strangest times …. It would be impossible for me to know what I want to say for each one for the whole year in January.

Depending on what I come up with, how I deploy it will vary (i.e. do a print and follow it up with a Facebook or Google ad to the same geographic area). For this reason as well, we are never sure when or what kind of listing we will have (IMAGINE HOW GREAT THAT WOULD BE IF WE COULD KNOW ☺). Having a smaller, more specific version of the calendar allows for more fluidity.

So, I would recommend one large plan with a general overview of what you would like to do and a smaller, more detailed calendar to work off of for a rolling three-month period.

PRO-TIP: Put reminders in your calendar of when you should start planning your three months, so you have time to plan and don't fall behind. For examples of my yearly and three-month calendars, please visit my website: jdconsult.ca

HOW TO MARKET
Your messaging, your deployment, the timing, and the mediums that you chose to use will depend on your target market, who you want your ideal client to be, and/or the ideal demographics for each listing.

All this is to say, there will be elements that should definitely stay the same from a branding/messaging perspective; however, there will be pieces or some messaging on pieces that change based on your circumstance.

Example: If I'm doing a Facebook ad to promote a property, I might have a catchy sentence that best describes the property, but my logo and my tagline always appear on EVERY piece. It's a both/and situation.

"Chill and put a record on in this former recording studio," is the catchy sentence, followed by my tag line: "Real Estate a different way."

When doing a smaller print piece, having my tagline might take away from the other messaging or make the piece look too crowded.

PRO-TIP: If you have a graphic designer to design your brand, during the design stage they will present you with mock-ups of the various pieces you are looking to have designed so you can see how it will all look. Use this process to determine if your marketing pieces will look too crowded with additional text or images. They should also give you a Brand Guideline Book. This book will show you how your logo, name, tagline, etc., should be used in various pieces as well as the acceptable fonts for your brand.

PRO-TIP: FIVERR has great brand designers at different price ranges if you would like to have it professionally done. This could save you thousands of dollars depending on your end goal.

REVIEWS

Reviews are a great way to market yourself in a very authentic way (as long as you allow your clients to post how they feel honestly). Referrals, word-of-mouth, and reviews are critical to people's decision-making process today.

Think about the last time you wanted to try a restaurant or purchase something. What did you do first? Look online? Ask a friend?

The same holds true for most real estate transactions. In fact, as per National Association of Realtors' (NAR) 2019 Profile of Home Buyers and Sellers: 51 percent of new buyers used an agent referred to them by a friend, neighbour, or relative.

Start collecting reviews as soon as you can. If you do something that wows a client halfway through the process, ask them if they will write a short testimonial for you (or if they are open to video, get them to say it on video right then!). Or if you are so inclined, write it yourself and get their approval.

This will do two things:

1. Get you a review.
2. Allow you to have reviews that speak to different themes. This will round out some of your various skills (so that people aren't reading the same message repeatedly).

PRO-TIP: When you receive a testimonial, ask the clients if they are alright having their name displayed. I often present them with three options in the hope that they pick one of them versus not having their name displayed.

This is an example of the email I send: "Hi X, Thank you so much for writing that amazing testimonial for me. I was wondering if you would feel comfortable with me posting this on my website or in some of my marketing materials. If yes, how would you like your name displayed?

1. Sam
2. Sam Bird
3. S. Bird

Thank you again!

Jen"

Where and how to use reviews:
Google reviews are great! I have also posted my reviews on LinkedIn, used them on my website, in my marketing materials, and sprinkled them throughout my Instagram.

PRO-TIP: I keep a word document with every testimonial/review I have ever received. I log their name, their testimonial, and how they want their name displayed.

PRO-TIP: I had my assistant group the testimonials into various categories to ensure I had a good mix on my website and my other online platforms. Once you start receiving testimonials, you will start to notice some trends and be able to break them up. Here are some that I noticed:

Neighbourhood knowledge
Knowledgeable
Negotiation skills

Patience
Great overall experience
Guidance

Collecting the reviews

As part of my "client process," at the end of (or during, if it works), I send out a communication to my clients asking if they would feel comfortable sharing their experience about working with me.

If I get a response, I thank them and then ask if they wouldn't mind posting it to whatever my preferred platform for that particular testimonial is. I send them an email WITH STEP-BY-STEP instructions and a copy of the testimonial in the email. Depending on the client, I will ask if they don't mind posting to a few platforms (Google and LinkedIn) or just one. I also share that I will send a gift card as a thank you for their extra time.

This has allowed me to gather various reviews.

Marketing pieces—the nitty-gritty

Now that we have looked at your brand, your messaging, and your plan, it's time to consider what works best for you and the best way to create and have them made.

Pieces to consider being made:

Business cards
Letterhead (paper and/or electronic version)
Return address labels
Listing presentation -
Buyer presentation
Notecards

Envelopes
Folders for your meetings/how you will present your pre-
sentation to clients
"Open House" signs
"For Sale" signs
Feature sheets
Mailing templates for when you have listed/sold a property

Depending on who you work with, your brokerage might already have templates to use for these. My question to you would be:

Do you want your stuff to look like everyone else's materials, or would you like to stand out? (See the section on branding.)

It's important for all your materials to be cohesive, consistent, easy to read, and easy for people to tell what you do.

Common mistakes
Business cards with way too much irrelevant information (various awards, slogans, advice, etc.) Photos that have nothing to do with what you do Outdated photos Business cards that look like they were printed on a home printer with perforated edges

Photography
I'm not sure why or how realtors started using their photos on business cards, on "for sale" signs, and letterheads. It's one of the only industries I can think of where we put pictures of ourselves where they are not needed. I'm not even sure if models have business cards with their faces on them, and they are legitimately selling themselves.

There is debate as to whether or not to use your photo in your materials.

Pro argument: Some people believe you are your brand, and therefore your photo should be everywhere.

Against argument: We are in the business of helping others; having our photos on a "For Sale" sign isn't going to sell the home faster. The perception could be that we are more interested in selling ourselves when, in reality, the focus should be on the home.

This will need to be as per your comfort level, and depending on what you chose for your brand; you might find having your photo in some locations (e.g., your website) and not others (not on your business card) is a good happy medium.

Photographers
There are various kinds of photographers. Verify that the photographer you choose specializes in photographing humans, or portraits versus another area. It does make a difference in the quality of the work.

The first photographer I used for my headshots specialized in product photography, mostly food. It can already be quite nerve-racking to have your photos taken; so, it does help to work with someone that can make you feel comfortable with the process and suggest options. My photoshoot with the food photographer didn't produce the best results. (I did NOT make that produce pun on purpose.)

Some photographers offer makeup artists and hairstylists to ensure you look your best.

Based on what your brand is going to be, pick clothes that fit into your brand identity and can be easily placed on those materials: that is, if you are going for a green background in your branding, wearing a red shirt might make you seem very "holiday" spirited. Consider wearing neutral, non-patterned clothes for ease of placement use on the marketing materials later.

I have also found that sharing your vision with the photographer in advance (or discussing a possible vision) will help with the outcome of the shoot.

Printing

This can be broken down into two categories:

1. The initial printing of materials
2. Day-to-day printing of materials

Depending on what materials you would like to use, you will need to find a printer to print everything (or various printers). These can be online printers that will ship to you or a local company where you might be able to see a sample before ordering your desired quantities.

Things to consider

Most print materials have different weights (aka thickness) and finishes (matte, shiny, semi-gloss).

PRO-TIP: Every printer prints colours differently. It's important to make sure that the materials you have printed match your brand colours and that there is consistency between the pieces. It would look odd to have your marketing materials displayed at a property where they are all different shades of the colours you want. First impressions are critical; it's better to put your best foot forward and have consistent looking materials.

What you choose will dictate the cost. It also can play into your brand. There is also a cost-benefit to consider: that is, if you plan to do a lot of mailings on letterhead, picking the most expensive paper can end up being costly. Likewise, a flimsy business card might not give the best first impression. Depending on your style and cost preferences, mixing different qualities might offer you the best of all worlds.

PRO-TIP: Ordering 5,000 pieces of letterhead might keep your costs low, however, will you be able to use them all besfore you decide to change your brand? Or do you have space to store it all? Perhaps, find a printer that could do smaller quantities when you have a specific project in mind.

Once you have your staples taken care of, the next thing to determine is how you plan to print the materials you might need for your day-to-day business operations such as marketing materials for listings (mailings, feature sheets).

One of the most challenging things in a busy fast-paced market is to coordinate timing when it comes to listing materials.

For this reason, it's helpful to have a printer (online or physical location) that you can rely on.

Many printers have the capacity to turn a print job around quickly—this generally comes with a cost—and others might need three to four days, but the cost is substantially lower.

Keep a list of your printers handy with their:

> Quantities
> Turnaround times
> Costs
> Quality of materials

PRO-TIP: Doing a big mailing? Costco is a great place to stock up on envelopes (the peel and stick ones) for a fraction of the cost of Staples. Stamps are a tad cheaper as well.

SOCIAL MEDIA

In this day and age, social media is essential to your business and goes hand-in-hand with a website. Clients will often choose to visit your social channels even before they visit your website. While building a community online is integral as a business owner, that doesn't mean you have to try to do it all. Start with what feels comfortable and manageable, and if it's an option, don't be afraid to outsource this to an expert.

Why should you use social media?
It's not rare that a potential client will find you on social media first, and that's ok because social media is a reflection of your brand (you and your personality, your offering/service, and your expertise). When someone clicks on your profile, they should know, at a glance, what your brand, as an agent, is about.

Social media is a great place to reach and connect with your current clients and community, while also being able to access untouched communities and potential clients who may have an interest in your brand. Each platform is a catch-all for your business because, in your profile, you can feature:

- **Bio** - Focus on one sentence to describe you/your business. Leverage this space as a call-to-action for your client. Entice them to take action with a question or a directive. For example, point them to a website resource: "Check out my Buyer's Guide."

- **Website** - Each platform has an option to include your URL in your profile.
- **Expertise/Value** - Your content should add value to your community. Whether sharing photos on Instagram or videos on YouTube, it's important that you are providing a reason for your community to keep coming back, just like you would to your favourite restaurant.
- **You** - I know, I know, it's not always the most comfortable thing to be in front of the camera, but as real estate brokers, WE ARE OUR BRAND. Try to show up in your content as much as you feel comfortable. Remember that people want to know who you are and build trust through these channels.

Another key aspect of social media is that it's a direct line of communication to your clients. This means that every engagement counts, so make sure you are replying to comments and direct messages in a timely manner. An engagement can be a written reply, an emoji, or even just liking a comment.

Which platform is right for you?

Social media has evolved to multiple channels, each of which offers unique purposes and value to your business. It may seem overwhelming to think you have to do it all, but it's not necessarily based on the goal you'd like to achieve through these platforms. Here are the four platforms that can support your business the best.

Instagram—It was built to be a visual platform and houses inspiring content. Instagram is now one of the most popular platforms for individuals and businesses. It is being used to share photos, short videos (up to sixty seconds), IGTV—longer-form video, Live, and stories— quick, in-the-moment highlights that last on the platform for twenty-four hours.

- **Useful if you like:** Great visuals and storytelling. Instagram has become a platform for telling stories through captions and sharing thumb-stopping photography and videos.
- **Benefits:** Instagram has many medium options through its multiple formats (feed, Story, IGTV, Live), so there is a multitude of types of content that you can create. Because of its popularity, Instagram is a great platform to increase your brand reach by building conversations and using hashtags to increase visibility.

Facebook - This is one of the original platforms, which means that it has the greatest number of users; however, the number of active users is decreasing. Facebook is known for connecting with friends, sharing photos, articles, links, and creating highly targeted business ads.

- **Useful if you like:** To share what's happening in your business with your friends. It's likely that you've connected with many friends over the years, and there is still benefit in leveraging this network. Also, if you're interested in creating business ads, this is the platform for you, as you are able to highly target each person.
- **Benefits:** Facebook is very multi-functional, offering you the ability to post to your personal profile or business page, create events, ads, and connect with clients through Messenger Chat.

Twitter - Was created to share quick, short-form content. Originally, each tweet (i.e. post) could only include 140 characters (now you can share 240 characters).

- **Useful if you like:** To stay up-to-date with current events and create a conversation with niche communities.
- **Benefits:** Twitter devotees are highly engaged, which means you have access to very targeted and niche communities. Twitter is an open platform, meaning you can interact with every single user and have access to all conversations.

YouTube—It is the original video platform, which now houses millions of channels, topics, and video types.

- **Useful if you like:** To share long-form video content. This is a great tool for house listing videos, market updates, and more personal, get-to-know-me videos.
- **Benefits:** YouTube is a great place to wow your clients if you have the capability to create an impressive video. This platform allows you to create multiple playlists in your channel so that you can group similar content together. Consider YouTube to help bring your clients along, while adding value in the market.

Tools to help you along the way

Content scheduling tools:

- Planoly.com
- Hootsuite.com
- Later.app

Design apps and tools:

- Canva.com
- Foodie—photography app
- Snapseed—photo editing app with all the details
- Inshot—video editing app

Not sure where to start? It can be intimidating. The social media world changes quickly. So unless you are already a pro or have an amazing amount of time to devote to it, hiring someone to help you or manage it all for you is advisable.

Aside from being current with all the trends, they will be able to help you:

- Create content
- Create a strategy with strategic goals

- Assess your key content pillars and key messaging for each
- Track and interpret response rates
- Switch directions when needed
- Help with ad placement
- Provide a different perspective, and/or guide you outside your comfort zone (if you need help with that kind of thing like I did!)
- Posting (maybe one of the simplest of tasks, yet it is something that is a total stumbling block for me). It sounds ridiculous, but I discovered I had tons of IDEAS. I got hung up on creating JUST the right message and getting it posted.

Having someone else manage that for me:

a) Gave me a deadline
b) Helped me get out of my own head and just post it regardless of whether it was perfect or not
c) Ensured that I was posting regularly which, as of now, plays a key role in the algorithms for viewership

PRO-TIP: Regardless of which social media platform you decide to pursue, one thing to remember is that this should not be your ONLY form of marketing. All social media is owned by "someone else" (i.e. owned by Facebook, LinkedIn, etc.). It's not your "property" like your website is. If one of the platforms were to become obsolete (hard to believe but it COULD happen) or if algorithms changed, or as people just naturally tire of one of the platforms, you could lose your base of "eye-balls." Having diversity in your marketing path is the best way to ensure that you can maintain a large audience in your future.

BUSINESS PLANS

Typically, a business plan is a document that outlines your product/idea, the competitive landscape, market opportunities, the financials, sales, and marketing, etc. While it's possible to create such a document for your real estate career, since you are not pitching for financial support from another source or a new product/idea, a lot of this content might be obtained from the marketing plan.

The one key element which is helpful to have is an idea of where your business will come from or where it has come from and how many transactions you need to do to pay your expenses and maintain a living. It's easy, when you see the size of one commission cheque, to forget that that whole amount is not your take-home amount. And as a result, you likely have to do more deals than you originally thought.

Here are the typical areas to review in preparing a real estate business plan:

> Your leads and transactions
> Average commission amount
> Average conversion rate
> Where your leads come from

The above are the traditional formulas that real estate agents have used to calculate how many transactions on average they need in a year to earn $X in income.

It also usually provides a good idea of how much lead generation you might need to be doing. Typically, the next step in this plan is to figure out how many people you should be interacting with on a daily/weekly/yearly basis. At the end of the day, this is still a "people" business, and we need to be with people in some capacity.

Given that so many real estate coaching companies still teach this method as a way of determining the kind of year you will have, it's probably prudent to follow what the "pros" are doing.

I will say it's good to have goals and something to work towards. The best thing that comes from calculating these numbers is that it gives you a very clear idea of the reality of work that's involved in your year. Pairing this with your budget (aka your expenses) might help you to push for those extra deals.

Some numbers to review:

> Total buyer leads
> Total seller leads
> Total listings sold
> Total buyers sold
> Total number of transactions
> The total amount of commission for the year

Average commission per transaction (total commission/number of transactions).

Example: If you did 16 transactions and your total commission was $125,000

$125,000 /16 = $7,812, which is your average commission per transaction.

The above is going to help determine what your next steps are:

Pick an amount of gross commission you would like to make in a year. This is your Gross Commission Goal (GCG).

To earn this, we need to calculate the number of transactions required:

GCG/Average commission
Example: $225,000/$7812 = 32 transactions required in the year to hit that GCG.

Another area that will help with your budgeting, marketing, and where you should spend your time to generate those leads is looking at WHERE your leads came from.

Source of Lead	No. of Sellers from this source	No. of Buyers from this source
Sphere/Friends		
Open Houses		
Past Clients/Referrals		
Geo Farming		
Print Pieces		
Sign Calls		
Your Website		
Agent Referrals		
Company Leads		
Social Media		
Others		

Once you have a year or two under your belt with numbers for the above, you can do a cross-reference against your marketing costs to determine an ROI for your various initiatives.

This is a great end-of-year activity.

Calculating your Marketing ROI
Have all your numbers ready:

What did you spend on the effort (i.e. print pieces, social media, online ads, client parties)?
How many leads did you generate from each?
How many sales did it generate?
What was the gross commission from this initiative?

An easy equation for calculating ROI is:

(Revenue − Investment)/Investment

Example: If you spent $1200 on a print mailing and generated one sale (with a gross commission of $7000)

(7000 − 1200)/1200 = 4.83

Multiply that by 100—to get the percentage: 483% ROI, which is great.

If you spend $1200 on online ads and generate zero revenue, it is not a good ROI.

NOTE: Some marketing tactics take longer than others to catch. Just because you didn't have any uptake on a particular initiative doesn't mean it's not worthwhile, especially if it's part of a bigger plan or bigger picture. The point of this activity is to monitor and be conscious of where you're spending your money. If you are spending $10K per year on Facebook ads and never generate any sales, either the messaging isn't working, it's not the right target market, or it just doesn't work. Measuring your ROI allows for more educated discussions with yourself or your marketing team.

PRO-TIP: Don't underestimate the value of your time with these initiatives. If you have to learn how to set up a Facebook ad and it takes you five to six hours, add that to the total cost.

Not all ROI measurements have to do with money. An ROI might have a different meaning, depending on what your initial goal was.

If your goal is brand awareness, the ROI has nothing to do with money. Measuring traffic to your website, email sign-ups, or social media interactions will be a better success metric. When you are constructing your marketing plan, add a note as to what the goal of the initiative is. Then when you are doing your end of year wrap-up, manage your expectations around the results accordingly.

WEBSITES

For setting up your website, you will need to look at the following:

1. Purpose of your website
2. Picking a URL
3. Buying the domain name
4. Hosting your website
5. Designing your website: use a template or create your own
6. WordPress, skins, plugins
7. Website security

Purpose of a website

Many agents have websites. Many don't. Many will tell you that no one actually visits their site. Others will tell you they get hundreds of leads a day from their site. A key driver to your website's success or number of visitors will depend on what you want, its purpose of being, and how much money you have to spend on it.

Online presence is important. Especially with today's market. What do you do when you want to learn something? Ask Google. The same is true for your potential clients. Having something of substance is important. I've had many clients tell me that they selected an agent based on their online presence.

The next step is to determine if you want to drive a lot of business to your website from external sources (increasing your original content, paying for SEO, etc.). This could cost thousands of dollars a month and could be hard to maintain. It could also be very lucrative for you.

Another option is setting up the website for verification and informational purposes. This is often what happens when you are running a referral-based business. This type of website isn't driving your business; it's supporting your business.

Trying to keep a website current can be a lot of work. If you have the financial capabilities to hire someone to do this for you, to speak in your tone, and make sure it's being updated regularly, this could be a great option. Keep in mind that there are hundreds if not thousands of realtors competing for Google space in your area. So, what will make your website stand out or make Google want to show it first?

When you are starting out, it might be easier (and more cost-effective) to have your online presence for informational purposes, and if you want to move towards it being a lead generator, do so after you have a feel of the market you are in.

Picking a URL
Determining your URL is an important step in building your business. A lot of this will come down to your branding. Is your brand you (Jendumitrescu)? A tag line (Sellingyourhomefast)? Something short (TTH)? Unless you have a very unique name like mine or pay a lot for Google rankings, it may not be easy to find you.

If your URL is too long:

- It could be hard to use on smaller marketing pieces
- Hard to work with when creating marketing collaterals
- Will people want to type the whole URL?

- Will it be easy to understand/read?
- Is what you are thinking about even available?
- Will there be typos as people enter it?

I have a really long last name. While that URL was available, I knew the risk of typos was HIGH. Which is why, for my business, I chose: jend.ca.

Buying a domain name
Pick a few names and then see if they are available. The most obvious choices are ones ending in .com or .ca. They are just more common.

Check to see if your domain name is available here: https://www.whois.com.

You buy a domain name from a domain name provider (or reseller). There are various ones, and they all charge various prices. Some will offer customer service should you require it while others won't. Personally, I have never had to contact my domain name provider, so this is one of those situations where cheaper is better.

PRO-TIP: Different domain endings will have different prices.

Length of purchase: If this is going to be your long-term business, you may as well buy it as long as you can. It saves you having to remember to renew it every year and the cost to fix everything should you forget to renew and someone else buys it. That is very, VERY COSTLY.

PRO-TIP: Enter the expiry date into your calendar the moment you purchase the URL, so you have a reminder to renew. If you have gone with a reputable reseller, they should send you a notification. I repeat, losing your domain name would really suck. Some might say it's even more costly than traveling with an expired passport.

What kind of domain to purchase?
You can either purchase a brand-new domain or an expired domain.

When you purchase a brand-new domain, search engines (like Google) put you in something called the Google sandbox. This is Google's way of making sure that you are a brand that is putting out relevant content and not trying to spam the internet. This is the reason websites do not receive a ranking right off the bat.

Exact match domains: Domains that match your business name. This makes it easier to rank because your keyword is already in your domain. Example: jendumitrescu.ca.

Expired domains: These are domains that someone has already purchased and used for their own business, but they did not renew ownership of the domain name. The benefit of these domains is that they could already have "domain authority" (which is like your website's reputation, and it contributes to your ranking). When you purchase an expired domain all their backlinks* and everything they did to acquire for the domain now belongs to you (until Google realizes it's a different business and removes the ranking that the other business had).

*Backlinks are links leading back to your site from other people's domains. Think of backlinks like citing a source. When they put up content that has your information, they link it back to you, giving you credit for your work.

The best place to find expired domains is expireddomains.net. You input the keyword you are looking for, and then you'll get to see the entire list of expired domains. Sometimes, you can find one that you can purchase outright, and sometimes people have them up for auction, meaning that you can bid against other people to get the domain you want.

How do you know you are purchasing a good expired domain? The backlinks are one factor, but then another way to check would be to look at Wayback Machine. This is a website that archives websites, and you can see what sites used to look like over time—the best way to check if it was a spam website.

Content management system

Now that you have your domain name (that is keyword friendly) picked out, it is time to think about your content management system (CMS). This is where your website is going to be and where you store all your content online. The most common types of content management systems you will see are WordPress, Squarespace, and Wix.

All these content management systems pride themselves on being able to quickly set up your website without having to code. Depending on what the purpose of your website is, you might require more functionality such as:

- Ability to embed your property listings
- Add a mortgage calculator
- Videos
- Area search functionality

You want to find something that is going to give you the best way to design your site with a lot of ease. Research all the options with these things in mind. WordPress (to date) has been the leader in this.

WordPress—It is the most recommended content management system. It has stood the test of time, and is where coders and developers come into play. WordPress has many themes and plugins that add different design options and functionality, which allow you to make the website look the way you want. A lot of the time, the free themes give you your basic functionality, and the purchased theme gives you more bells and whistles to make all the changes you want.

PRO-TIP: Buying a theme that allows changes will increase the speed of your site since you will have to add a lot of 'extras' in the background to make everything work the way you want. Remember, at the end of the day, your site's speed is critical to user experience.

WordPress Plugin—This is a piece of software equipped with functions and code that can be added to your site that adds new functionality without needing to hire a developer. *Disclaimer on plugins: Not all of them are created equal, and having too many can slow your website down, so it is better to do your homework to see what you want your website to do and plan your plugins around that. Also make sure to remove any plugins you aren't using.*

Hosting

After choosing a Content Management System (CMS), you need to decide who you are going to host with. If you choose a CMS like Squarespace or Wix, they will also handle the hosting of your site. But if you choose a WordPress site, you can use sites like SiteGround or WPEngine. These different hosting platforms also allow you to purchase the domain name and security certificate (SSL), which provides you with a one-stop-shop for all of your website needs.

Security

When you purchase a domain, you are also going to want to purchase an SSL certificate. What is this? It is your website security certificate. Google has named it a ranking factor in its algorithm. In the top left corner of your browser, there is a message that pops up, letting you know if the site is secure or not.

Not only is it important for you to have your site secure for ranking purposes, but it also protects your information and, more importantly, it protects your information from hackers or Man-in-the-Middle (MitM) attacks. These are attacks directed at insecure networks. Safety first!

PRO-TIP: Despite having a secure website, your content can get stolen. Meaning, people can just copy and paste something that you have written.

There is not much you can do about the latter. However, a good tool for searching for copied or duplicated content is https://www.copyscape.com.

<u>Site speed</u>
When you have a slow website, it affects your website search engine ranking because not only does Google not like it, your viewers don't either. If your site loads slowly, chances are that a potential client or customer has already hit the back button, going back to Google. Google doesn't like it when people don't stay on your website; it looks as if your site isn't solving their problem, and your site will be lowered in the rankings.

PRO-TIP: You want to make sure your website is very responsive (that means FAST) on phones and tablets and gets a high ranking from Google. In order to do this, you need someone who knows what plugins to use at the backend of your site to give you the functionality you want, but that also doesn't affect your website speed.

Example: The first website I built (or rather had someone build for me) had so many different plugins, and they weren't all compatible. Result: super slow loading speeds, hence Google was not a fan of my website, which resulted in lower rankings.

This is obviously a very technical topic. The key point I would like to draw attention to here is this: Ask questions and know some of the basics so you can have an educated discussion with a developer.

Check with your friends or other realtors if they have a good developer they can recommend. Check out other websites that have been built by your developer. What are the speed test results? How accessible are they? Are they able to provide support once it's built, or will you have to find someone else to manage that for you?

<u>Website accessibility</u>
Is it easy for you or other people to access your website?

Example: I will often have my marketing team load listings or blogs on my website. Having a site that is built-in WordPress (a more universally known backend platform) will ensure a higher number of people can help you out when you need it. Or better yet, maybe you know how to do it. (See the section on delegating.)

SYSTEMIZING YOUR BUSINESS

We have all been given the same amount of time in a day. As a self-employed person or the owner of a small company, it's important to be as efficient as you possibly can. Your time is money. And if you are hoping to have any sort of work/life balance, there is absolutely no point in being inefficient with common tasks. There are many benefits in systemizing as many parts of your business as possible:

- HUGE cost savings
- Allows you to scale/grow your business
- Time saving
- Frees you up to focus on money-making activities
- Allows you to easily share tasks or delegate as necessary with new staff members
- Allows you to maintain a consistent customer/client experience
- Eliminate errors/mistakes
- Protects you legally
- Create a mindless business flow
- Allow your business to be run how you would like it to be run without you always having to be present (which means more or BETTER family/vacation time for you)
- Working with better employees—ones that align with your vision

In *The E-myth Revisited*, Michael Gerber talks about why most small business owners don't make it past five years. I would encourage you to read this book if you are interested in learning more about the benefits and how to go about systemizing your business). To summarize (and this is a VERY short summary): Self-employed people are good at the job that they started out at. If you are a caterer, you are likely to be good at preparing and presenting food. When it's just you, you know exactly what needs to be done. The type of food to be ordered, how you determine quantities, the process of preparing each dish, the quantities of ingredients for each dish to ensure maximum cost efficiency, billing, set up. . . . As you can see, there are tons of little details that are likely in that person's head. As they grow, and hire more staff, without processes in place, they may be able to teach that specific person the way to do the job just like them, but as they scale bigger, person #2 is going to teach person #3 their way, person #3 will teach person #4 THEIR way. . . and then, the next thing you know—your business might not be recognizable to how you initially started it or how you intended it to be. What Michael Gerber suggests is this: If you build processes, the way you would like things to be done, and maintain a binder (old school—but whatever format you choose to use—you get the point) of those, you will ensure that your business is being run consistently and in a way that you are aware of. It's not about control in a bad way. . . but think about it: As a caterer, you understand the importance of maintaining food costs and the presentation of your creative delicacies. You would like to make sure that even when you are NOT in attendance at an event, it's being done in the way that best represents you. It is, after all, your company.

The other thing that having processes does is that it allows you to hire based on the person you feel is best suited for the position versus someone that can do the job. If all the processes of a job are documented, you could essentially give "the best person" for the job the training manuals, and they can learn how to do it. Because they are the "best" person, they might bring more to the table. Hiring someone that can only do that job might mean they don't or aren't willing to bring more to the table.

As with anything, there is always room for improvement. By hiring the "right" person for the job, they will take the task as is, and after a while of performing it that way, be able to come to you with suggestions on how to improve it. It can be a discussion between the two of you and something you are a) aware of and b) agree to. Which is a win-win situation.

How to write out your processes
One of my first jobs after university was writing ISO procedures and policies for companies. ISO stands for International Organization for Standardization. This organization helps with the following (quoted directly from their website):

> ISO International Standards ensure that products and services are safe, reliable, and of good quality. For business, they are strategic tools that reduce costs by minimizing waste and errors and increasing productivity. They help companies to access new markets, level the playing field for developing countries, and facilitate free and fair global trade.

Basically, my job (this was in a manufacturing company) was to document how the company was run. I would meet with the various departments and determine all the various tasks they performed and document them. The idea being in theory (and this is a very simplified description): Every single step of every single task should be documented in a way that any person (I, as an example) could go and perform that task.

This eliminated any confusion as to HOW things were supposed to be accomplished, and also in training time, since everyone had the opportunity to read and reference the various tasks if required.

While this was not the most stimulating job I have ever had (let's face it I much prefer DOING versus WRITING), it did teach me the importance of having every task of my real job documented.

This became very handy when hiring admin assistants:

A) I no longer had to rely on my memory for everything I needed to teach them.
B) It made hiring people less daunting. Hopefully, you haven't experienced this, but if you have, you know it can take a while to find the right assistant, and the thought of constantly having to train someone new can make even the most efficient person say, "Oh . . . do I really need one? Maybe I can just do everything by myself."

Different processes I have created:

Administrative weekly to-dos
Administrative monthly to-dos
Seller processes: pre-listing, listing process, after the deal
Buyer processes: steps from the first contact to after their closing

Processes for any activities that have more than five steps: My accounting systems, database operations, client management processes, new buyer systems, all the elements of a listing, how to place an order with my commercial printer, preparing bulk mailings, etc.

If you look at all my processes, you would see that my entire client experience—every little step from entering their birthday to their pets or kids' names—is mapped out. This is what ensures that every client has the SAME experience. And that no matter how busy I am or where I am in the world, each step is still followed.

PRO-TIP: Keep all processes in Dropbox/cloud by category. Administrative, buyer processes, seller processes, etc.

PRO-TIP: If you are using a task management tool or your database to manage the buyer and seller processes, be sure to have another backup somewhere—should you change systems or if something is deleted by mistake.

PRO-TIP: If you have emails that are regularly sent out, keep those templates in one place so that the email doesn't need to be created each time. My database allows me to create processes, and as part of a particular step, there is a way to attach an email template, so when I arrive at that step, all I need to do is press "send." It's very efficient.

DELEGATION

Super producers automate and delegate.

The name of the game is efficiency. They say that it's the two-minute tasks that will eventually eat away into your day and your productivity. So being mindful of where you spend your time and how you spend your time will ensure a greater success rate for your business.

As a self-employed person, we often feel like we need to do everything because after all, "It all comes out of our pocket," so the financially responsible thing would be to handle everything.

I can tell you that this will lead to full-on craziness and absolutely no work-life balance. Not to mention, it will end up costing you more in the long run. Here's why:

1. If you have to learn a new skill to be able to accomplish the task, this is time you are not spending making client connections. For example, learning how to deploy a social media ad may seem like a five-minute Task. However, the algorithms are constantly changing as are the trends, so unless you would like to spend a large

portion of your week brushing up, this might be a task that's better handled by someone else for you. Or not done. It will depend on your marketing plan/business model. Yes, it will cost you to pay someone—but their one hour of work could be equivalent to five hours of your time. One is a business write off, the other is time spent away from your work.

Another common example (for real estate agents specifically) is around "picking things up", i.e. a deposit cheque or condo documents. Unless it is REALLYs only a half hour or legitimately on your way, this is an activity better suited to a courier service. MOST offices have a courier service that can run small tasks within your city. (If they don't, why not ask about setting one up?) Generally, I've found that most pick-ups/drop-offs are under $20. If I was to do the same task, it could be an hour or an hour and a half out of my day PLUS gas, PLUS parking (if it applies).

2. Being a Jack-of-all-trades generally leads to being a master of none. AND to massive BURN-OUT. The kind that can lead you down deep, dark bad holes. Where there is lots to be lost.

To calculate if a task is worthwhile, calculate your hourly wage. Take what you want your annual salary to be/hours worked.

Two things to keep in mind:

- The gross amount of money you make will be different from your net after your expenses (another reason to make a budget and a business plan)
- There are no consistent hours in real estate (unless you are extremely diligent). Monitor your hours (like honestly write down how many hours you work each day for a month). This might surprise you because you will realize that you are not working as many as you think or you are working way too many and require more automation or delegation.

Then calculate your hourly rate.

If you would like to make $100K a year, depending on your expenses, you might need to make $150–$200K a year.

> Example: If you work 40 hrs/week (50 weeks/year), your hourly wage is $50.
> Example: If you work 60 hrs/week (50 weeks/year), your hourly wage is $33.

It's your life; it's your lifestyle. You do what works best for you. This is just part of calculating the big picture of how to run your business in the most efficient manner so you can make the money you want and lead the lifestyle that brings you the most joy. Because being self-employed can be hard, you should feel like it's worth it at the end of the day. Throughout my career, I've generally heard that any task that is $100 or less should be done by someone else. The more money you make, the more this could change. So re-evaluate every so often.

More isn't always better
As you can see from the above example, working more doesn't necessarily translate into more money in your pocket. So how do you maximize?

The easiest first step is to have systems and processes. Then look at all the various tasks in your day or with a transaction—all the two-, five-, or ten-minute tasks that are taking away from your big tasks. The ones that only you can perform.

Do you need an admin assistant? Obviously, there are various factors to consider before going down that path. Having your processes in place and all the tasks documented will definitely make the transition from being a solo entrepreneur to having an admin assistant a lot easier. Not to mention the mental block some people face when giving up control or wondering what the admin assistant would do. Many small business owners know they need help; however, they hire help before being ready, and it doesn't always work out. I'm not suggesting you don't hire someone before you have everything set up (because then it might never happen, and the reality is that the admin assistant might be able to help you identify tasks). I do suggest spending some time preparing. There's balance. And the goal is to keep admin assistant replacement low.

One thing I've noticed in the past few years, and in particular when I was trying to hire an admin assistant, was that the skill set I was expecting them to have was probably not realistic. Or not realistic for the salary. But actually, I just don't think it was realistic. Let's break it down:

I wanted someone that was organized (OBVIOUSLY), detail-oriented, articulate, had an ability to problem solve (thinking outside the box and bringing me solutions versus just presenting the issue), technologically savvy (aka: understand my very, very confusing database at the time), able to manage Instagram, run my Facebook ads, search for trends, manage my website, write blogs, be able to constantly adapt to new projects while still getting the mundane, boring monthly to-dos (like entering addresses into said confusing database) AND be able to keep up with the thousand ideas that come to my head, and enjoy working basically by themselves.

I recognize it would have taken a very *special* person to keep up with my thousand ideas. But other than that, can you see how all the above tasks kind of call for different people?

It's been my experience that someone who is very creative (therefore being able to manage the marketing, the writing, the trend searching) is likely not someone who is going to be satisfied entering hundred addresses into a database.

This is where I really had to break down my delegation. And what I have been preaching for a while—we don't want to work with a jack-of-all-trades (master of none). I want someone who REALLY loves admin work— and all that comes with that specific job—to be my admin assistant. And I want someone who LOVES to keep their finger on the pulse of Instagram, marketing, or design trends to be managing that side of my business.

In enters the concept of having various people working WITH you. (Notice, I didn't say FOR you.) This is something that I feel is a more sustainable model for the one-off self-employed person or the duo/partner team.

Having various people in various areas

This model can end up saving you a lot of money and headaches because you are not hiring for a role that isn't fillable. You are hiring or contracting people who are specialized in the field in which you want them to be AND when you need them. (Lots of agents wonder: What will I do with my admin assistant during the non-peak times? Will I have enough for them to do?)

Here's how I did it. I hired:

1. A virtual assistant
2. A company to manage my social media (with a lot of input from me)
3. A marketing designer (I'm lucky because my awesome office has a killer marketing team. I can create ideas, and they design them for me. You can also hire an independent designer)
4. A website designer/manager
5. A photographer and videographer for listings (they edit the photos and ensure they are properly sized for all marketing mediums). Any other tiny edits could be done by my marketing designer
6. A professional floor plan creator (usually my photographer could do this but if yours doesn't, there is no need to spend hours measuring all the rooms in a house when there is someone else who can put together a professional drawing for you)

7. Caterers, or staff for client events—to take care of the activities so I can be with my clients

<u>Where do you find people?</u>
For the first three positions, there are many online freelance companies where you can hire someone for a specific or short-term job/task, hourly jobs (like you need one hour of research on a specific topic), or on a more permanent part-time basis. Example: Fiverr, Upwork, Freelancer.com.

With these services, you post a job, what you would like to pay, and then people bid on your job.

You find everyone from graphic designers, website designers, content writers, and bookkeepers, to virtual assistants. Take a peek to see what else! Some of these companies also offer help with payment issues (should there be any) and a time tracker (for your peace of mind).

There has also been an increase in companies offering virtual assistants (V.A). The biggest struggle I've had with these companies is their response time. But maybe that's just me. I've had much better responses by contacting V.As directly through the above-noted freelance sites. However, the hourly costs are higher.

There are many different things to consider when you are hiring a V.A. If you hire them directly (through one of the freelance companies I mentioned above), you will have an opportunity to read their resume, reviews about past work completed, and, in most instances, (through the website) be able to arrange a video interview.

If you hire them through a V.A specific company, the pricing model could differ. You may or may not be able to "video" meet them; you may or may not be working with the same person every time.

Ask lots of questions

One company I spoke with offered me a real estate specific V.A. who would be able to proficiently handle all client communications in English. And an accountant who was fantastic at book-keeping and QuickBooks but would not be a great fit in client-facing activities. The hourly rate was also quite different.

When I hired the V.A from Upwork, I arranged to work with her on that platform until we both felt like we trusted each other, and then we moved off the platform. (They did charge a service fee for all hours worked.) I arranged to pay her weekly after she submitted an invoice with all her hours. She was with me for over a year and a half. Similar to other assistants I worked with, I did encourage her to take additional training that she felt would benefit her AND the work she was doing for me. I treated her like an assistant, and it built a better working relationship between us.

Here are some things to consider if you are going to have an assistant/ V.A (that you wish to keep with you for a while) and depending on their skill set:

- Have them join in some training groups, so they are properly trained versus you are just sharing what you know/think. LinkedIn Learning has some great training modules across a variety of topics.
- Have weekly meetings with them. This is a great way to manage projects, and to ensure that things are getting done and in the way you expect. I found having weekly meetings also allowed me to delegate more tasks. I was able to share little things that were in my head. And of course, as time passed and they became more comfortable and proficient in the role, I was able to offload more.

PRO-TIP: I would have video meetings in lieu of phone meetings. Seeing each other face to face can be very productive.

- Have a central location where a task list is kept (google docs spreadsheet or a task management tool), so everyone is on the same page about the task, deadline, and progress. This will save you time and from having to always ask, "Hey, what's happening with XYX?"
- Depending on where they work (at an office with you or at home) they might like some social interaction. This can be in the format of a video conference with you, or through group training. Ask them so you can be mindful of their preferences.
- Use systems like Slack to organize photos and reduce the number of emails and keep a better thread.
- Create a shared calendar; either give them access to your calendar or create a shared one. This allows them to manage consumer expectations and also know when and how to reach you. It saves you time and effort when trying to coordinate meetings.

PRO-TIP: If you would like to just work with one calendar, use colour coding, so they know the difference between work versus personal time block.

PRO-TIP: I had my V.A enter her appointments (or times when she was not going to be available) in my calendar to help manage my timing expectations as well.

Delegation around communication
Proper delegation can dramatically increase your efficiency. While not directly considered "delegation," being more deliberate with your communication and how you communicate with people can also save you a lot of time and unnecessary back and forth.

1. What is your fastest way to communicate? There are so many ways to communicate today: text, email, WhatsApp, Instagram, direct messages, phone, Facebook Messenger, etc. Managing all of them can be time-consuming. However, from a client perspective, it's important to communicate in a format that works best for them.

For me (and again I'm probably old-school and WAY too practical), phone is the fastest and most efficient for conversations. Text is great for when you need short answers; however for me, typing on the phone can be way to time-consuming, not to mention, that when I'm driving, I can't answer anything. I do recognize that sometimes it just needs to happen. I've found two solutions to this. (a) I'll use the dictate function (and, of course, check for any typos or any dictate "whoopsies" before sending). (b) Since I am a PC user and iPhone user, I purchased an iPad with the keyboard accessory. This allows me to type responses much quicker than on my phone.

While you might have less control over the communication format, if you can be mindful of which ones you are not as strong at, you might be able to make some changes, as I have done. If you are a two-finger typer, maybe the "dictate" function will be more efficient for you.

2. Using in-between time to your benefit. Whenever I am in a taxi, on public transportation, or waiting for a personal appointment, I have my iPad with me so that I can still answer emails or text messages efficiently. (Looking back on my education, I would have to say that grade nine keyboarding was probably one of the most useful courses I have ever taken. Did I just date myself by saying that?) It's portable, small (fits in my purse), is fully connected to my Dropbox and Gmail, and connects easily to the internet. Making use of these small moments means less big moments required when I get home.

PRO-TIP: During super busy times, when I'm driving a lot, I will often call my assistant, and I have her type responses to emails that would normally need my direct attention. That way, I'm using the time in my car efficiently and still answering emails that I only might have the information for.

3. What you say. Eliminate a lot of back and forth in emails and texts by providing solutions or options that work for you. So, if

you are looking to schedule a call or meeting with a client, suggest three times that work for you add a sentence saying, "If none of these work with your schedule, are you able to reply with two other options?" If you are still unable to come to reach a time that works, maybe a quick phone call can reduce all the back and forth.

The 4-Hour Workweek by Tim Ferriss has some great tips on how to better maximize your time. I listened to the audio version driving. Because I like maximizing my time!

DATABASES

Coming from a sales background (before my real estate career), I can say that databases are key to your success. Back in the day, people used to keep binders with a piece of paper and everyone's contact info. In today's fast-paced world, this just won't cut it.

Databases serve many functions:

1. Keep all your contacts in one spot
2. Allow you easy access to connect with your contacts
3. Provide great follow-up options if you are not skilled in timely follow-up
4. Help ensure an excellent client experience for your clients. AND THIS IS KEY to building a successful referral-based business
5. Track your contact with them
6. Keep key details that will make them feel very valued
7. Free space in your mind because you don't need to remember everything

There are many real estate specific database companies. What they offer varies, as do their price points. There are Canadian companies and there are American companies. The American companies might offer more functionality. I have also learned that they are still quite "American" based, so this can cause some problems (i.e. a lot of their terminology is not the same. For example, Closing versus Escrow, so you might find yourself not being able to use it as easily as you would like).

I've also found that some offer the basics of contact management, and others help with project management. If you are looking to streamline the different programs you currently use (database, mass email system like mail chimp, project manager like Podio) you will be searching for a more robust database.

The key is just to get started. So pick one that feels right and is the most user-friendly based on your personality.

Here are my suggestions for figuring out which database is right for you:

1. Ask fellow agents in your office what they are using (and by using I mean—do they log in and use it daily or just pay for it monthly).
2. Contact the companies and ask for demos. Ask them what they are best known for, where they hear their customers struggle.
3. Price points.
4. Customer service (trust me you will want help with this).
5. How easily do they sync with your email/calendar system?
6. Can you customize fields for your client info:
   Kids' names, ages, pets' name, anniversary dates, birthdays, their favourite books, restaurants, etc?
7. Is it easy to see when you last had contact with the client?
8. Do they make suggestions as to who you should contact? Based on what parameter? (Is it last call, last note, last text? Do they track text messages?)

How to fill your database

Most companies offer an import tool where you can import all your contacts from whatever existing platform you use. I would advise doing a clean-up of your contacts BEFORE you do the import. Regardless of how easy they say it will be, there are usually errors and fields that will need cleaning up. The less you have to clean up once it's imported, the more free time you will have to do other things.

PRO-TIP: Budget some time for this. Don't do it when you already have a million things on the go. Doing this right the first time will save you lots of headaches and inaccurate information later on. Plus, having an accurate database will make those first mass communications so much easier.

PRO-TIP: Be resigned to the fact that database clean-up will always just be a thing on your task list.

PRO-TIP: If you have already been in business for a while and have a good number of contacts, pay someone to do the data entry and clean-up. There are "task-oriented" websites where you can pay someone for small tasks. *(See the Delegation section.)*

PRO-TIP: Send out a communication (or better yet, call people) and let them know you are in real estate and looking to keep in touch. Use the contact point as a way of verifying their information.

PRO-TIP: If you are looking to send mass emails, verify how the database you are looking at will send them. Some databases will deploy the messages individually (even though you are sending a mass message, the system will send them as an individual message so it won't appear as spam (in most instances), and hence you will have a higher delivery rate.

ACCOUNTING

You are running a business. The only way to truly measure your success (and to make money to survive) is to be able to track your revenue and expenses.

Commissions − Expenses − Taxes = Profit

Most agents have NO idea what their expenses are. This is a critical part of your business. Real estate flows quickly. Large sums of money come in and go out at the same pace. It's important to know where that money is going. Because the only way to increase your PROFIT or your take-home $$$ is to make sure your expenses are managed and your taxes are as low as they possibly can be.

I'm not an accountant, so I won't be able to dive into the ins and outs of what you should be doing from a tax perspective. Still, I can suggest ways to save yourself a lot of time and hassle as it relates to being organized with all your paperwork so the accountant can take over when need be.

There are many elements to accounting in real estate:

1. Keeping track of your expenses
2. Budgeting
3. Flow of money
4. Year-end accounting
5. Credit cards

Keep track of your expenses
Some agents believe in keeping all their receipts in one box and then hiring a bookkeeper at the end of the year to input everything into a format the accountant will work with. I've found that **managing things monthly** saves the year-end dread most people get when they know they have to get organized. And it can save you some money (reducing expenses is key).

When I first started out, I had someone design an Excel spreadsheet for me with the various categories. I would enter in the amounts from each receipt onto individual Excel sheets, and they would automatically get pulled over to a master sheet broken down by category. This allowed me to see, at a quick glance, what my expenses were relative to what I had budgeted for.

Times have changed, and now there are programs like QuickBooks and other online platforms that allow you to scan your receipts into the cloud and have your credit card bill or bank statement fully incorporated.

Here are some online money management tools:

YouNeedABugget
MoneyMinderOnline
QuickBooks

They all have a cost associated with them. And if you have read my other sections, you know I support this. Because, you get what you pay for.

PRO-TIP: Before selecting an online money management tool, do some research:

- How protected is their online storage system?
- How long will your data be kept in the cloud?
- What happens if you need to extract that data? (That is, if you were to get audited.) What format does it come in?
- Can you create a budget? How easy is it to see your yearly totals in the budget?
- Does it connect with your bank accounts and credit cards?

PRO-TIP: Think long-term. Where will this company be in six years should you have an audit? I tend to stick with the larger name companies because they could have a higher likelihood of being in business longer. Especially a company like QuickBooks. And the cost isn't that much more.

For my receipts, I use a program called RECEIPT BANK. This program allows me to:

- Scan receipts with my phone. They are automatically uploaded to the cloud and into QuickBooks.
- Any receipts that are emailed to me, I can forward them to a specific email address and have them uploaded into QuickBooks.

This has saved me SO MUCH SPACE. I no longer have to keep paper copies of receipts (thus paying for storage or using up other valuable storage space in my home), and I take photos of my bills every few days. This reduces the amount of work I have to do all at once with my receipts. QuickBooks has a similar program.

PRO-TIP: Regardless of how you want to manage your receipts, be sure to write who you were with or what the receipt was for (Gift for X), so it's very clear what it was for. This will save you a lot of hassle down the road (in a few years) if you are ever audited and need to recall what the receipt was for.

PRO-TIP: I keep track of every meal, coffee, or client visit in my calendar. Not only does this help with daily time management, you will have a reference of your activities should you need one for an audit.

PRO-TIP: If you are not using a calendar that allows you to go back in time, print copies off monthly and store them with your receipts.

Car Mileage Log

Any commissioned salesperson who uses their car for work should be keeping a mileage log. The Government of Canada suggests that the best way to get the full benefit of your claim and to support that your vehicle was, in fact, used for business is to document for each journey:

- Date
- Destination
- Purpose
- Number of kilometres driven

There are various ways for you to keep track of this:

- Manually writing down the above in a notebook (kept in your car)
- A note file on your phone
- A mileage tracking app (NOTE: there are free and paid versions for this. Similar to what I have written about accounting/receipt programs—decide what is best for you based on ease of use, whether they would be admissible by the Canadian Government, and how long the information is stored if you can download the transactions and keep for your own reference)

PRO-TIP: If you are a QuickBooks customer, they make a mileage tracking app which is connected to the rest of your accounting. This would definitely make things a lot easier.

PRO-TIP: Take a picture of your odometer on the anniversary of your lease/purchase date each year. I file this photo in my "Expenses" Dropbox folder for each year as proof. I also try to get the time and date to show up in the photo (to further support and track the total amount of kilometers that were driven each year).

As per the Government of Canada Website: After one complete year of keeping a logbook to establish the base year, you can use a three-month sample logbook to foresee business use for the entire year, as long as the usage is within the same range (within 10 percent) of the results of the base year. Businesses will have to show that the use of the vehicle in the base year remains representative of its normal use.

PRO-TIP: If you use more than one vehicle (two different cars in your household, and you drive both), a log must be kept for each one.

Budgeting
Budgeting allows you to be intentional about your money. It allows you to:

Plan— for current expenses and other unexpected ones.

Control—not spend money you don't have. Because there is no consistency as to when we are paid as real estate agents, having control and being aware is a great way to ensure you don't go bankrupt.

Save—having an idea of what your annual expenses are versus your annual income will give you an idea of how much you can save a year.

PRO-TIP: Many money management books will suggest you pay your "savings" account like it's an expense or has money automatically withdrawn monthly as a type of forced savings.

Set goals—when you understand your expenses, you are better able to see what it is you need to earn to live the lifestyle you want. Knowing your expenses is a critical part of your business plan because it will help determine how many transactions a year you need to be making or what dollar amount you need to bring in yearly to maintain your lifestyle.

Use your profession to further your personal wealth—I've heard many a millionaire say that owning real estate is the way to substantially increase your personal wealth. The idea being: the more properties you can acquire (good properties) and collect rent on, you will have someone else paying your mortgage, and eventually, once the mortgage is paid off, you will have a constant stream of income for yourself. Not to mention a large asset portfolio should you require funds once you retire.

However you choose to invest your extra funds, the point is that you need the extra funds first. And the only way to get them is to be diligent about your expenses, your income (through the business plan), and having a budget to get you there.

<u>The best way to set up a budget</u>
If you have never kept track of your expenses, START NOW. Like literally, right now. Create a document that has business expenses on one side and personal expenses on the other. Write everything that comes out on a monthly basis under the appropriate column. Look at your bank and credit card statements to check for pre-authorized or recurring payments. Plot them accordingly. Don't forget to put rough estimates for some of life's necessities that often go unaccounted for, like coffees, groceries, miscellaneous expenses, and small cash purchases you repeatedly make.

Decide how you are going to keep track of receipts and the type of expenses moving forward.

When you have a receipt, allocate it to a category. Maybe you could start out small with only a few categories for now and then add more as and when you feel ready.

Example:

Work categories: Office, marketing, taxes, car, entertainment.
Personal categories: Home, food, entertainment, personal care.

If you are more experienced and have had some sort of system to your accounting practices, review what your expenses were last year. Break it down by categories and assign a similar value to it this year. Moving forward, assign receipts to those categories, so by the end of the year, you will have a more accurate sense of where your money is going.

The goal of this exercise is to see where you might have opportunities to save money. Many people have lots of subscriptions to monthly services they no longer use or can be combined with other programs. Creating a budgeting system is often the first time many see just how many recurring payments they have.

PRO-TIP: Getting your whole accounting system up and running can be daunting. Go easy on yourself. If you are starting from scratch, implement a few changes that seem manageable for you. Once you feel comfortable, add some more. If you do too much, the whole thing might come crashing down (unless you thrive in those kinds of situations—then go for it!). And that is not the goal.

Examples of expense categories:
Dues/subscriptions
Brokerage fees
Office rent
Phone
Insurance(s)
Car—payments
Car—insurance
Car—gas
Car—maintenance
Parking
Computer/internet
Postage/delivery/courier
Marketing—advertising
Marketing—direct mail

Marketing—website maintenance
Marketing—social media
Marketing—print/brochure
Marketing—promotional items
Marketing—Staging
Marketing—other
Listing prep
Subscriptions
Office supplies
Education expenses
Client entertainment/gifts (maybe separate this out for client parties versus meals with clients)
Travel expenses.

Flow of money

It can be hard, for most people, to control finances (especially when you are running a business in addition to your personal expenses) from one bank account. It's for this reason that many fiscally responsible business owners create various bank accounts. Part of having a budget is knowing where and when payments need to be made. It's being in control of your finances versus your finances being in control of you.

When you have different accounts, you can transfer money accordingly to each so that you know where you stand with all your expenses rather than having a lump sum of money in one account that money is just deducted from. With the latter, you can never be sure what is actually yours to be spent versus what needs to be budgeted for expenses.

There are various equations as to how these bank accounts should be set up. Here is a loose template:

1. Income (incoming money)
2. Expenses (business expenses)

3. Checking account—personal
4. Savings account
5. Tax savings

PRO-TIP: Some say it's best to have your savings and tax savings account at a different bank to remove the temptation of easily being able to use those funds.

Determine what amount you would like to be saving and the percentage of the money that should be going into your tax savings FROM EACH DEAL, and every time a commission cheque comes in, allocate those immediately.

This is in line with the "pay yourself first." Then you take control of the distribution of funds and ensure that money is set aside in each account versus taking what's leftover at the end of the month.

Below are some great resources to check out:

Profit First by Mike Michalowicz This is a book on accounting, budgeting, and how to manage your finances and plan for the future. Michalowicz's company also offers financial trainers. He says, "Consider them like your personal gym trainer—but only for finances. Someone to help you stay accountable and on track."

Brian Buffini's podcasts or coaching. Finances are a huge element of the Brian Buffini coaching program.

Wealthy Barber and Wealthy Barber Returns by David Chilton. This book discusses the concept of paying yourself first.

Budgeting and Canada Revenue Agency (CRA).

Accountants know best. But here are some things to be mindful about when it comes to your taxes and planning for tax season.

Plan for taxes. Putting money aside from each commission cheque, so you do not need to come up with one large sum at tax time, is likely the best option. It can be harder said than done. One option is to put a portion of the funds directly into your "tax" account (see notes above about the separate bank accounts). If you are worried about being diligent about doing this with every cheque, some brokerages offer the option to hold back funds from your commission cheques on your behalf. Think of it as forced savings. Or, you can't miss what you don't have. If this is your first time being self-employed, having your brokerage manage this for you might be the easiest way.

Either way, save the money. And/or pay the instalments. 'Because, trying to catch up on both (a lump sum that's due plus instalments for the coming year) can be very taxing. (Ok, that was a bad joke. . . but you get the point)

Life Happens . . .

Despite our best intentions, sometimes things just happen, and you are not able to pay what you owe. CRA does have a collections hotline. And they, for the most part, are happy to help you come up with a plan to repay. Being proactive and contacting them will likely result in a more positive repayment plan (versus waiting until they find you!). It can seem scary, but taking that first step is probably the hardest part.

Credit cards
As with most topics in this book, how you choose to manage your credit card(s) will be entirely up to you. And since most credit cards offer rewards, plans, or points, user preference will depend on your end goal with your desired credit card program.

The simplest way is to have one card dedicated to all your office expenses and one for personal. If we all did that, this could be the shortest chapter in history. The flip side is that if you are going to be putting lots of business expenses through your credit card—why not make it work for you?

I will use myself as an example in this chapter.

I love to travel. My credit cards are geared toward collecting travel points. Through all my years of work (both corporate and personal), I've been able to obtain many free flights (taxes not included, of course).

I have a Visa and an Amex. Both are travel cards.

I like my Visa because:

- It is accepted almost everywhere a credit card can be accepted.
- I earn points for dollars spent in addition to kilometers travelled on partner airlines.
- I'm offered travel insurance and travel benefits.
- If need be, I can carry a balance.

I like my Amex because:

- I earn MORE points per dollar spent.
- The travel benefits are more extensive.
- I have purchase protection (good for when you are making large purchases).
- It is generally a great customer service experience.

Because Amex is not accepted everywhere, I prefer my Visa as my primary card.

Because the majority of my credit card spend is work-related, I prefer these two cards for point accumulation.

My preference is NOT to carry a third card (which would be my personal card) because I just don't want three cards, and to always be carrying them around. As a result, I need to be more diligent with my monthly accounting. It's a trade-off for sure. As I mentioned at the beginning of this chapter: one card for work and one card for business is the easiest way. I like my free(ish) flights more than having separate cards.

PRO-TIP: Loyalty can really pay off. Whether it's with a cell phone company, your bank, or your credit card. The longer you are a good standing customer with the bank, the higher the likelihood that, should you require help, they will value you and do what they can to help you. NOT EVERYONE, but since I've had my credit card for over twenty years, when I have a favour, they will try to accommodate. For example, if you lose your card or it's compromised, replacement speed is key. Sometimes that loyalty can pay off. ***This is my own personal experience—not something that is guaranteed.

Obviously, the higher the benefits, the more expensive the credit card. So the choice is yours.

PRO-TIP: Some accounting programs will allow you to create "rules." So if you visit a specific grocery store or clothing store and pay with your credit card (or bank card), you can create a "rule," so those particular expenses are tagged as "personal" and accounted for as such. This can save you some time (and money) if you do choose to have one card instead of two.

Year-end accounting
Depending on if you are incorporated versus a self-employed contractor, "year-end" could be at different times. If you are self-employed and your year-end is December, I've found a great practice is to use the month of December (this "quieter" time of year versus the busyness of the spring or fall market) to finalize all your accounting for the year.

There are a few benefits to performing this activity in December:

- Time: This process could take a while. Normally there are less "immediate" real estate tasks that need to be completed in December.

Tackling this task in December versus at the height of the spring market, when taxes are due, will dramatically reduce your stress.

- Memory: Every year, there are bills or payments that I didn't tag properly or were done as online payments. This can be particularly true if your credit card is used for both personal and business activities. Chances are you might have a better recollection (and if your memory is failing you, not more time to research) what those payments were for the sooner you do it.

PRO-TIP: Doing your accounting on a monthly basis will alleviate all of the above. But if that isn't your style, December is a good second option.

Things to finalize in your year-end:

Are your personal and business expenses completely separated?

Break down your business expenses by categories. Different parts of your business will have different claim allowances.

Make sure that all items charged to your credit card or withdrawn/paid for from your bank account are accounted for.

Ensure that any major expenses are accounted for: child care, medical expenses, RRSP contributions, donations.

If you are keeping paper copies of receipts, gather all receipts and file/store them in an easily identifiable container/box.

Do you have a reputable accountant to use? Have they worked with real estate agents in the past? How do they charge their clients: hourly or flat fee?

If you work from home, notify your accountant. They will ask you to determine what percentage of your home is "office." And any associated fees with that (annualized): internet, mortgage interest, hydro, condo fees (if applicable), property tax, home insurance, mortgage insurance.

PRO-TIP: Some accountants are paid by the hour; the more organized you are, the smaller your final bill.

PRO-TIP: Hiring a virtual assistant (and one that specializes in an accounting program such as QuickBooks) could save you a lot of money in doing your monthly or year-end account reconciliations. Some quotes I have received range from $13–$20 per hour. And what they can accomplish in that time is more than most agents do and could be a better use of your time. This will also reduce your accounting bill. It's helpful if they are familiar with your province's tax laws for inputting purposes.

TOOLS TO ORGANIZE
YOUR WORK LIFE

I'm about simplicity. The less I have to manage in terms of tools, apps, programs, the better. And so far, I've managed to get through years of real estate by sticking to this. There are a few that have been so critical that I feel they are important to consider.

There are so many different programs depending on what it is you would like to do. And since programs/apps are always changing and evolving, I figured it would be better to list some areas where apps could help, and some of the basics that I feel are great at providing a good foundation for running your business. Of course, what you choose to use and the direction you take with these programs/apps are going to depend on the level of your business, what you are good at, how much support your brokerage provides, etc.

Suggestions:

Gmail: Good for email, calendars, meeting invites, worldwide accessibility, and sending documents. With Gmail, you also get access to Google docs, sheets, photo sharing (think of the Microsoft suite of services: Word, Excel, etc.) but in a cloud format that is easily shareable.

PRO-TIP: Using a neutral platform like Gmail (versus a product that is unique to your computer or cell phone, i.e. Apple Mail) will provide flexibility over the years if you change the computer/phone brands.

PRO-TIP: For all my listings, I create a "showing feedback" document in Google sheets. I put every showing in the "sheet" and my latest action with the agent: that is, if I have sent them a text or email requesting the following. If the agent responds, I put their comments into the "sheet" and share a link with my client so they can get the feedback on what I have been doing. I have found that when the information is delivered through a "third party" source, and they can read the comments, they better understand the realities versus having the words just come from my mouth.

Cloud-based document storage: The very first thing I would encourage anyone to do is start backing up all your files to the cloud. I can't tell you much stress this has saved me. Not to mention time, convenience, and did I mention sanity? Depending on if you are a PC or MAC user, there are different options. As a PC user, I'm partial to Dropbox. I also just use this to store ALL my photos (work and personal). (I've been doing this from times past, even before I was an iPhone user.) I also pay for iCloud backup on my phone so that, should anything happen to my phone, I'm able to restore it to the way I was using it before (hopefully).

I've also found Dropbox to be particularly helpful on showings. I now store all the MLS listing sheets in my clients' folder in Dropbox and access them from my phone during the showings. It's better for the environment too.

Google Drive: This is another great resource that would be accessible regardless of your platform or location.

PRO-TIP: Pay for extra storage. It doesn't cost much, is a business write-off and will save you so much pain if your computer crashes. And it's not like you can go back in time to get all the documents back …

PRO-TIP: Saving all your listing photos to the cloud will ensure that you always have them. Sometimes, photographers send photos with a link that only allows access for a certain period of time. I always download ALL versions (high, medium, and MLS resolution) into my Dropbox. This is handy if you ever need to create marketing pieces with various listing photos or create a memento for your clients: that is, a photo book.

Electronic signing programs: These have become a legal way to sign real estate documents. This has definitely changed the way real estate is done: no more waiting for a fax and having to recreate documents destroyed by said fax machine. These programs also facilitate signatures from various parties (in a clean easy-to-read way).

PRO-TIP: Before using this, make sure you are legally allowed to in the region where you trade real estate.

PRO-TIP: Only certain programs are considered "legal." Make sure that the one you choose is—then there is no need for unnecessary headaches with your regulatory board. The legal programs have a stamp next to the signature for authenticity. Example: DocuSign or Authentisign.

I've personally had a lot of success with DocuSign and appreciate their customer service. That's definitely something to check.

Storage/transaction rooms: These cloud-based "rooms" are a place where you can safely store your secure documents related to a particular transaction. Here, you can give certain people (client, lawyer, mortgage broker, or admin staff) access to this virtual room to view or download documents as necessary.

They also allow you to have your entire team on board with your task list from lead to close. It takes file storage to the next level. Example: DocuSign transaction rooms.

LastPass: I LOVE this tool. It enables me to share access to different programs/websites that I use with others by NOT revealing my username and password. This is great if you have an assistant or are using a virtual assistant. I was able to share all of my websites with them, and they never once had access to my passwords. LastPass also gives you the ability to immediately revoke access should it be required.

Project/task management tools: As you will learn in the systems part of this book, systemizing your business will make you a more customer-centric agent AND will give you a chance to have some personal time. Using project management tools will help you to rely less on your memory and more on getting the job done well. Checklists make for smoother transactions and relationships, ESPECIALLY when you have twenty balls in the air.

These tools also allow you to coordinate or assign different tasks to different individuals.

Example: If you have an assistant and certain tasks that need to be completed during a listing, these tools allow you to ensure that no task is missed and that each one is properly assigned. For example, Asana.

Group communication platforms: These are a great way to streamline communications with various people in real time. These apps/programs generally allow you to send files/photos in a more compressed format so that all information with regard to a particular topic is contained in one location for easy reference. For example, Slack.

Backup/external hard drives: Call me old-school, or maybe I have just had too many computer issues, I'm all about the double backup. In addition to Dropbox and iCloud on my phone, once a week, I also do a physical hard drive backup. It's set to run every Monday, and while I have never had to use it in the past seven years, just knowing it's there provides a big sense of relief. Years of photos, memories, real estate transactions (that you legally need to keep for a certain period), all my expenses. . . Why not just take that extra little step. Minor inconvenience = major cost savings.

PRO-TIP: By having everything backed up electronically, I've been able to dramatically reduce the amount of physical office storage space I require. It makes for a much more streamlined business experience.

Backing up text messages:
A lot of communication these days is done via text message. And many people don't think about how that could affect them later, should they need to reference a particular conversation. It's possible I'm going to sound a bit repetitive here, but make sure to back these up. A colleague of mine was once taken to court for a work-related issue, and having the backup of the conversation was the saving element. Depending on your phone, find a solution that works for you and your life.

Personally, I have found using WhatsApp a better tool for communication as it seems to compress images and data in a better format, so you use less storage space on your phone. Again, this is a personal preference.

PRO-TIP: Use backup programs that run automatically and frequently. This will save you from having to remember and thus forgetting. Always be prepared (as the girl guides say). Preparation saves time and hassle later.

Tech support: Unless you work for a company that provides you with technical support, invest in a way that will. With every iPhone I buy, I purchase the Apple Care—two years of unlimited tech support, when you are self-employed, can really take a load off your mind. Not to mention if you drop, break, or drown your phone, the re-purchasing is often way cheaper! (You will likely cover the cost of AppleCare just in that savings alone.)

Having this option plays a major factor in my phone purchasing decision. The same could hold true for your computer, printer, or other technical devices in your life, which are critical to your day and productivity.

For computer support, research a company (in advance, so if you need them and your computer is broken, you have the info stored somewhere where you can easily access it) that can do the same with your computer if you are as un-tech savvy as I am.

Some other categories to consider when running your business:

Photo editing programs—for use when posting to IG or for blogs on your website.

Screen sharing programs—aids in discussions with your clients.

Stock Photography—great websites to obtain photos for you to use for your website, social media, or marketing pieces. These can range from free photo sites to pay-per-use. The quality also differs.

There are many tools available. It's best you look at your organizational preference and use the tool that's best for you.

PRO TIP: Yes, there are free systems for probably anything you want to do. I encourage you to look at the big picture. There is a reason these systems are free. Either they are not as robust, or their true potential comes at a cost.

What you want to avoid is having to "change" programs/tools at a later date because that's when costs (your time) became higher. Not to mention your inefficiency with the learning curve to learn new programs and /or have your assistant learn a new program. I have yet to meet a free program that I haven't had to switch from or suffered through ads or eventually needed more from.

PRO TIP: Running too many programs/tools/apps is going to clutter your life. The name of the game is streamlining and simplifying. That is going to reduce your costs overall and help you run a smoother business.

Cell phone plans

Cell phone plans are changing all the time. At the most recent glance, some of the larger companies are now offering unlimited data. This topic is going to be one of personal preference and will largely come down to the lifestyle you lead. If you are the kind of person that is generally in a Wi-Fi zone and/or doesn't travel much, your needs are going to be different from someone like me, who does like to travel and uses Waze all the time to get around town.

A few things that I feel are important to point out here:

1. *Additional discounts:*
    Your real estate board might offer additional or preferred discounts on cell plans. Check if they have a specific contact for you to be in touch with. I found I was able to get a better price on the phone and other perks, such as increased data (this was before unlimited became an option) and additional discounts.
2. *Traveling:*
    It's been commonly said (and I have experienced it first hand) that the minute you go away on vacation, that's when you are going to do a deal. (This is a fantastic problem to have: EXCEPT if you are paying crazy amounts of money to use your phone. I have learned in some of my travels that not all hotels/countries have great Wi-Fi. For example: On more than one occasion, I've been to Mexico where "FREE WI-FI" is promoted. What I have discovered is that it means

"in the lobby only." Your room is basically a bunker. Unless you have your own data plan, having to go to the lobby and competing for Wi-Fi is never desirable, especially if you are in the middle of a deal.

3. *Roam Like Home:*

   Roam Like Home is a program offered by some cell phone providers. This program allows you to have access to your "regular" cell phone plan abroad. Meaning: if you have unlimited data in Canada, you will have unlimited data in that country (***if that country participates in the program—check with your cell phone provider). This could save you hundreds of dollars! Let's play out two different examples.

Traveling WITHOUT Roam Like Home

It's advisable to purchase a travel plan of some sort to avoid crazy costs. If you arrive at a destination that doesn't have great Wi-Fi or you are not able to access it on a regular basis, you will likely blow over that pre-purchased plan and then be charged for data overage, which can be super expensive OR in a worst case scenario, your cell phone provider is a more local company, and you won't be able to access your data plan in the country you are in at all unless they have Wi-Fi.

In years past, I've had $500 cell phone bills for going over my "pre-purchased plan," and that often happened in the first few days (we use way more data than we believe). For the remainder of the trip, I was stressed and unable to use my phone unless I was in the hotel room. Research how much it might be without Roam Like Home and if there are no caps as to a total monthly cost**

Traveling WITH Roam Like Home

You have freedom. Freedom to use your phone how and when you want. Which means, if you are trying to do a deal and still take a tour of that museum that's been on your bucket list forever, you can actually do both. And not worry—you will not be broke when you get home.

PRO-TIP: Re-negotiate your plan often. Most contracts (if you purchased a new phone) are two to three years. Check in periodically to see if there are any better deals. Sometimes, if you are getting close to the end of your contract, they will be open to changing your plan. If not, mark your calendar for the end of your contract date and then call. Given your contract has expired, they might be more keen to keep you and give you a better deal.

**NOTE: Plans can change all the time and it's best to check with your cell phone provider. The above are just meant as examples of things to consider with your plan.

HOW TO GET NEW CLIENTS

As with most industries, there are two types of clients—ones that are brand new or referred.

There are definitely many different ways and activities to generate clients within those two streams. For example, working open houses, hosting home buying or selling seminars/webinars, lead generation companies, a strong online presence, social media, involvement in your community, cold calling, or becoming a neighbourhood expert with designated marketing efforts in one area.

Communication with your sphere

It's commonly said that working with a client that has been referred is much easier than trying to earn the trust of a new client because they are already "warm," meaning they have been introduced by someone who can be trusted. Fundamentally, working with a referred lead is way more efficient to your bottom line versus trying to convert a cold lead that has never worked or heard of you before.

Everyone is going to have a way that works better for them. What's important here is to understand the difference between the two and how it can affect your bottom line, the amount of energy required, and, ultimately, the likelihood of being able to lead them to a successful sale or purchase.

Many studies (both from Canada and the United States) indicate that most business in real estate is referral based. Naturally, people ask friends and family if they know a good realtor. Depending on your network, you might be able to build your business purely on this model or use a blend of both streams. How you get clients will also largely depend on your marketing plan (see the marketing plan section)

There are many different real estate coaching programs (reference the coaching section) that can enlighten you on the various ways to get clients and the best way to build out a business plan to support that method. Having a plan and something that feels comfortable for you and works well with your personality type will help you stick to that method, and it will let your natural personality just shine, which is important in an era of being authentic. Not jumping all over the place in terms of methods will also save you time, energy, and mental capacity. Ideally, by figuring out your client acquisition method, you can then also build your business plan and, subsequently, your marketing/social media plans. Doing this will already put you light years ahead of your competition. There is only a small proportion of agents that are this organized. And given that you are reading this, I'm going to assume you are looking to make sure you are on the path to being part of the 20 percent that earn 80 percent of the money.

How to get new clients—PART II

Once you have determined how you would like to acquire a client, part two of the equation is converting that lead to a client, and eventually guiding them to complete a transaction with you. If you are new to sales, or have not had training in this department, it would serve you well to learn, practice, or seek professional help in the area (see the chapter on coaching. There are many sales coaches who will dive deeper into this topic, depending on how you would like to build your business). As I mentioned earlier, sales has changed and most people are not looking to be sold TO anymore. They are looking for a guide. Once you have been introduced to a potential client (which is a great feat on its own) it would be a shame to lose the opportunity to turn them into a client because you used some old-school techniques.

A few quick tips:

1. Listen. We were given two ears and one mouth for a reason. People want to be heard. This is not an opportunity to sell yourself. It's their transaction, not yours.
2. Ask well-thought-out sincere questions.
3. Take notes.
4. Ask clarifying questions.
5. Know your audience. This goes back to listening. If you are working with a couple that would like to one day have a baby, showing them a one-bedroom condo in an elevator-less building because you think it's outrageously cool is not going to demonstrate you heard or intuitively considered their future.
6. Be sensitive/aware of people's emotions.
7. Confirm follow-up actions.
8. LISTEN.

Learning to sell (or guide) well is an art. And one that requires much more detail than I can go into here. Building that trust and connection with someone is what will set you apart. It's a process that is constantly evolving and a skill that is always in need of fine-tuning.

I'll leave this section with one story. A few years back, I was car shopping. I had three dealerships in mind. It's not a process I enjoy and so I was very deliberate in my process and admittedly, I tested each of them (although they probably weren't aware that I was doing that).

1. Did they ask me what I was looking for?
2. Did they hear what I was looking for?
3. Did they offer me options based on what I was looking for?
4. How easy did they make the process for me?

Because I wanted to expedite the process, if they failed step #1, I told them.

I wanted:

a) A car that handled well in the snow.
b) Had a great sound system and easy connectivity for music.
c) Was comfortable, easy to drive.
d) I had NO desire for extra fluffy things. Zero. Nada. A car with the above that was a nice colour was fine by me.

Dealership #1: Did everything well. Let me ask questions and answered with just the right amount of detail. He also went over and above to facilitate an EASY car delivery. Which was not part of my initial requirement, but because he listened, he picked up on a concern that was arising for me and found a way to make it stress-free.

Dealership #2: Before beginning the test drive, the sales person walked up to the car, popped the hood, and started to explain the engine to me. FAIL: There is an expression in sales: "Know your audience." At no point had I indicated that I had any interest in the engine or what it looked like. He was doing what he had been coached on versus actually listening and ADAPTING to what my needs were.

Dealership #3: Addressed each of my requirement during the test drive and then ASKED if he could explain some other features. He could sense (being emotionally aware) that sharing other features, which were not of concern to me, might have fallen on deaf ears. By asking my permission, I felt he heard me and respected my desire for this to be a quick process. BONUS POINTS: He sent me a follow-up note by mail. The ONLY one to do that. Which went a long way.

In the end: I went with Car #1 because I enjoyed everything about the process and the car the most. Car #2, which was cheaper, didn't get a return visit.

In my opinion, sales isn't about getting someone to spend more or pay more; it is about earning a customer. Which is why it's critical to have a skill set (and ears) that allow you to do that.

COACHING

For many, being self-employed is a whole new world. Whether you are coming from a job where you had someone you reported into or from another industry, it can be daunting to try and figure out:

How to start?
What should you be doing?
How to build your business.
Best daily activities.

Working with a coach can help give your day direction, help set up the right habits to build you a solid business, create accountability, act as a sounding board, boost your confidence, offer suggestions, and help you avoid what is often called the "drift." Real estate, despite being a people business, can be somewhat isolating, especially if you don't go to an office every day.

The drift happens when you spend too much time by yourself, in your own head, and not collaborating with others in the industry. Even if you are someone that plans to visit the office daily, it's sometimes difficult to chat and learn with other agents as people are out and about or (worse) not open to that concept.

If you have already been in the real estate business for a while, coaching can rejuvenate your passion, help your overall performance, and offer new techniques or strategies to address areas that you are struggling with.

Overall, coaches force accountability. And for anyone looking to be really, really successful, in any field, accountability is key. Whether it's work, sports, personal goals, having someone to share the highs and lows, give you goals to work towards, readjust the course when necessary, and generally know you have to check in with them is going to push you forward. There will be days when you don't feel like doing what's necessary, but knowing you have a goal will inevitably move the needle, even if it's just a bit, when things are tough. And when you look back in a few months or at the end of the year, you will have always accomplished more.

There are MANY, MANY different kinds of coaching. Over the years, I have had the pleasure of trying various styles.

There are real estate coaches, each with a slight variance as to how to run/build your business:

- via referral
- online leads
- converting new clients
- scripts/dialogues
- cold calling/door knocking

Coaches that guide in specific areas:

- negotiating
- social media
- body language
- emotional intelligence
- having difficult conversations

(Just to name a few.)

Coaching can be short- or long-term. Generally, I have found that getting started and finding your groove with a coach can take a while. Depending on your work style, it would take a year before you see progress or can better hone your skills. Be patient; settling into the groove can reap big rewards versus continually changing course. Slow and steady wins the race.

Having said that, if you don't feel good working with your coach, it can be just as detrimental as never staying the course. Some personalities just don't mix. If that is happening, ask the coach how they are feeling about the situation or explain that you would feel better suited to another coach. As I say to my clients all the time, "Chances are if you are not enjoying working with me, I feel the same, and it's better for everyone's interest for us to change things up. I would be happy to refer you to another trusted colleague that I feel you might be better suited to." Having honest and open discussions will only serve you well.

PRO-TIP: Before committing to a coach, spend some time chatting with them. Ask them what their working style is, how do they motivate their clients, how have they handled situations where their clients have not seen progress? See how you feel just speaking with them. NOTE: the coach is not meant to be your friend. So there may be things they suggest/say that you don't feel like doing; this is also the point of coaching—to push you out of your comfort zone.

PRO-TIP: Many of the larger coaching companies will offer one-day or two-day seminars where you can get an overview of their methods and coaching techniques. This is an excellent way to try out various programs before fully committing.

The point is: learning is growing. The more you learn, the better your business will do. Real estate is full of opportunities to learn, take courses, and attend seminars or conferences. Over the years, you will gain a better understanding of what you need to grow and improve your business.

If you are the kind of person that just doesn't vibe well with receiving direction from others, I would suggest that maybe the right coach hasn't come your way OR you are better suited for a different kind of learning. Whatever your style, I do encourage you to be open to the concept that learning and growing is really key to life (as reported by many of the top-earning business owners).

Dialogues

I've worked with many coaches over the years, and it was often suggested to have "dialogues" ready for different situations with clients. Dialogues are sentences, questions, and solutions to common things that buyers or sellers ask or question us about.

Example: "Why should I hire you versus your competitor?"

Dialogues provide a good base to work with because I do think it's important to be prepared. If you are new to real estate, it's helpful to have some standard answers in your repertoire so you can confidently answer questions, versus stumbling along in a conversation. Having dialogues also allows you to formulate an answer that might be more client-centric.

While I do see instances where dialogues are valuable, in my opinion, there are a few caveats:

1. Practice them. Repeat them in a mirror, so you see how you look. You want to avoid looking like you are just regurgitating the information. If so, you will break trust and appear fake.
2. Understand the general concept. If you are able to do this, you will be able to generally respond in a more natural way and adapt some of the key principles, so they fit well with your situation.

3. In the age of authenticity, clients will likely pick up very quickly on anything that looks like it's a standard answer or that it's been memorized. Listening to really understand what your client needs will take you much further in life.

4. Practice. I think this is important regardless of the meeting. It never hurts to review the questions you would like to ask at a meeting and/or, depending on what you have learned in previous discussions with the client. Go over the key points you should be discussing with them. Often, I've seen agents go through an entire presentation without asking any questions or even paying attention to the reactions from the clients they are meeting with. Having interactions, being able to ask questions, and learning AS MUCH as you can about your client's concerns, worries, fears, and things that are important to them is going to help set you apart from other agents and, in the long run, build a better relationship.

To summarize: Dialogues can have a time and a place and are definitely a great place to start if you are new to the business. It's a technique that has been around for a long time, so use it carefully. Remember: the point is NOT to be like every other agent. Take care with that face time (and by face time, I mean the physical time with your clients) with your clients; use it wisely and sincerely. People rarely like to be sold to. They want to be understood. Being smart with your language and reactions can ensure this. I've found that there are many general communication tactics, empathy, negotiation books/podcasts, or seminars that might provide much better guidance on how to communicate with your clients than spewing out an over-practiced dialogue.

CONFERENCES

Similar to coaches, there are TONS of different real estate conferences you can attend, both in Canada and in the United States, varying in topics and ideas.

There are general conferences which cover:
Real estate topics
Business topics
Industry updates
Motivational elements

Other conferences are more tailored to:
Technology
Social media
Marketing
Business ownership

I started going to some of the big generic real estate conferences, attending the various coaching day seminars and then, as my skill set or my desire to learn different elements grew, I started branching out to other non-real estate related industries—more business-focused ones to ensure I was keeping my eyes open and my finger on the pulse. Plus, as they say, the more your business grows, the more you will pick up things that previously were not relevant.

STAGING

I firmly believe that staging a property is key to ensuring your client sells their home for the maximum amount of money possible. Not every client will want to, and there are definitely different degrees of staging: from styling to full house turnover. In the staging world, there are a few different elements:

1. Stagers: Some can help you style or stage a full property either with their own products or from renting furniture, and suggesting the client buy some accessories.
2. Furniture rental companies: You can rent furniture for a period of time. They have everything from couches to mirrors and accessories.
3. Stylists: They use your clients existing furniture/accessories and make suggestions on items to remove or reconfigure in the home.
4. You can have your own inventory (either stored at your home or at a rented storage space).

The question as to whether you use a stager and either pay for their inventory, rent products, or keep your own inventory is going to come down to ROI calculation—how often are you listing properties and what your tolerance is for being able to coordinate all the moving pieces of a stage.

Here are some pros and cons for both.

Pros of hiring a stager:

- They do everything—movers, coordinating setting everything up, ensuring it's picture-perfect, disassembly.
- Depending on the stager you use, you could have a more current inventory, which can make your listings seem more current and appealing to buyers.
- Less overheads.
- Less time required from you.

Cons of hiring a stager:

- The initial upfront cost can definitely be higher.
- You are subject to their schedule/availability. So if you are offered a last-minute listing, it could be tricky to coordinate.

PRO-TIP: Have a few stagers on hand for the different levels of staging to help if their schedules are busy.

PRO-TIP: If the design is important to you, ask to visit one of the stager's recent projects (if they do not have an up-to-date website).

PRO-TIP: Every stager has a different process in terms of how they work with the client, their billing processes, staging time, and disassembling time. The more you know about their process, the better you will be able to manage your client's expectations, and that can really come in handy.

Pros of doing it yourself:

- Less costs. Potentially. It will depend on the number of listings and your overall yearly cost to purchase, store, and maintain all your inventory.

Cons of doing it yourself:

- Depending on how many listings you have in one year, your inventory could become stale.
- More time is required to coordinate all the details: storage, insurance, movers, set up, tear down, being on-site to coordinate.
- You spend time shopping to rotate inventory.
- If you have various listings at once, you will need multiple items. At other times, the inventory just remains in your storage facility.
- Decorating is a skill. Unless you have a talent in this particular area, the final result could be disastrous.

PRO-TIP: NEVER leave price tags on purchased items that you plan to use to stage. It seems basic, I know, but you would be surprised at how many times I see homes with price tags on. It's horrifying. If you do not feel comfortable keeping your purchases or even removing the stickers, hire a professional stager. Nothing says cheap and is more visible than Homsense price stickers everywhere.

PRO-TIP: Consider sharing all the staging costs with another coworker. This could have some of its own complications, but if you are able to make it work, it could provide cost savings.

PRO-TIP: Staging includes not only the furniture but all the smaller items such as plants, decorations, art, towels, soaps—everything to make the home look like it's lived in.

INSURANCE

One topic not often discussed (and certainly not mentioned in any of the real estate training courses I took) was how to protect yourself in the long run. When you work for a company, in most instances, you are offered health insurance or coverage and disability coverage (short-term and/or long-term) should you become ill for an extended period of time. If you have never worked for a corporation, it's possible you are not aware of these benefits.

NOTE: Insurance options will be different by province.

There are various types of insurance you might want to consider:

1. Health insurance
2. Life insurance
3. Disability insurance
4. Critical illness
5. Travel insurance
6. Car insurance

1. Health Insurance—or extended health coverage. This would reimburse additional expenses that are not generally covered by provincial health care: prescription drugs, hospital expenses (and/

or provide more hospital room options), dental, and other medical expenses. Purchasing extended health coverage on your own is never going to be the same as if you were under a plan with a large corporation.

Example: My coverage offers me a $25 reimbursement for extended health care (physiotherapy, massage therapy, etc.) up to a total of $400/year per practitioner. When I worked for a company, I was given a total of $500 for each practitioner. So if each visit was $80, I was reimbursed the full amount up to $500.

Obviously, each plan is different. And the costs are going to vary based upon your personal health history and the type of coverage you like. Depending on how you plan to use the health coverage and the costs purchasing, this may or may not be of value to you. Do note that plans never improve; the longer you wait, the more the value decreases. Also, the healthier you are, the easier it will be to qualify.

Another benefit of this health insurance is dental coverage. Dental upkeep can be costly, and yet it's very important to good health.

Finally, this insurance can offer many benefits that you might not even know you need at this moment. For example, life-sustaining drugs, emergency air ambulance services, hearing aids, artificial limbs or other prosthetic appliances, home care, vision care, etc.

PRO-TIP: Being in good health will be more beneficial to you when applying for insurance policies. Since most people tend to be in better health, the younger they are, some could say it's best to apply as soon as you can. They will request a full health history from you.

PRO-TIP: If you are just getting into real estate and coming from a corporation that provided health coverage, check with that provider if they have a "transfer' program"—a program where you can continue coverage on your own (a personal health insurance policy) with them. A benefit to this is that, in most instances, you would automatically qualify versus having to do all the tests and see if you meet their requirements.

2. Life insurance: This protects loved ones should you die prematurely. Having life insurance can help replace income, pay debts, and create or add to an estate.

    Life insurance can be purchased based on the desired level of income you want, who you are supporting, and outstanding debts (mortgages, car payments, etc.).

3. Disability insurance: This insurance can be short- or long-term and provides financial support while you are unable to work. For example, if you are required to have an operation and will be off work for a few weeks, short-term disability would help cover some of your lost income. This insurance could start anywhere, from a few days to a week, after you submit the claim. The long-term disability is for a more prolonged absence. The amount of payment you receive will be calculated based on your salary.

    This insurance could be included in a health insurance plan.

4. Critical illness insurance: This will ensure that you and your family are covered in the case of a life-changing illness. Unlike life insurance, this policy pays out during your lifetime. So it can help cover some of the costs that could arise. It is a one-time, tax-free payment that is triggered by the development of specific diseases or conditions.

    Life insurance is paid out after you pass.
    Disability insurance is triggered by an inability to work (so it's work-related).

    Critical illness is paid out based on developing a specific disease or health condition.

5. Travel insurance: If you never travel, you can skip this paragraph. If you do, please read on.

    Travel insurance can be purchased through various sources and for different periods of time.
    1. Most travel agents offer insurance for purchase for the duration your trip.
    2. Many banks offer insurance also for purchase for the duration of your trip.

3. Credit cards (mostly the travel ones and some Amex cards) have travel insurance as part of your plan (for no additional cost). There may be a maximum number of days you can be insured. Check before you travel.
4. Most health insurance plans have a travel component.

Always verify how long your coverage is valid for. If you are going for an extended period of time, it might be necessary to purchase extended coverage through another provider.

NOTE: Your provincial insurance might have a restriction on how long you can be out of the country and still have valid health care.

PRO-TIP: Take a photocopy of the policy and emergency numbers to call. Give it to your travel companion, so they know what to do in case of an emergency. I also store these documents (and all my travel documents) in Dropbox. This way, if I lose the documents or they are stolen, I have a backup.

6. Car insurance: Car insurance is mandatory in most provinces. If it's not mandatory where you live, I would HIGHLY recommend it. It's just smart. Full stop. One thing most real estate agents don't consider is that they are transporting clients. Contact your insurance company to find out if you should be insured in a different capacity. And if your liability amounts should change. Most policies offer $1million in liability coverage. Realistically, if you were in a very bad accident with a client in the car, $1 million won't go far, especially if you are at fault. These are just things to consider. And things that are not discussed.

PRO-TIP: Your board or organization might already provide coverage for you in some of these areas and/or have a group policy that you can join for better coverage and/or reduced cost.

PRO-TIP: Keep a record of all the policies/coverage you do have in one location, so should something happen to you, the information is easy to find by your loved ones. I keep these with my will—all in one place.

BUILDING A GOOD NETWORK OF SERVICE PROVIDERS

Having a good network of service providers to contact is key to providing an excellent experience to your clients, both during the process as well as after. This will also make your life way easier. Real estate can happen really quickly, so if you have someone you trust that you have built a good rapport with, it can mean the difference between winning a listing presentation or a house for a buyer versus not.

Examples of people to have lined up in your service portfolio:

Real estate lawyer
Mortgage brokers
Stagers (various decorating styles and ones that style/consult versus ones that will perform the whole stage)
Painters
Contractors
Someone that performs small maintenance tasks (depending on where you live, there could be a company where you can hire people by task and by the hour. This is a great alternative for small jobs, such as installing a light or repairing a toilet. Example: JIFFY)
Plumber

Cleaning service

Movers

Home insurance company

Landscape company

Junk removal

Professional organizer

PRO-TIP: If you have a few suggestions for each provider (especially the ones that the client will be working with directly), they can have a discussion with each and choose to work with the one they feel is best suited to them. This means it's THEIR decision not yours. Our job is to suggest rather than tell.

Not sure where to start looking for these service providers? Ask other fellow agents or even some of your existing clients. Maybe they have someone to recommend.

Interview or meet with new service providers before referring them to your clients. Get an idea of how they work and how quickly they respond to requests. What is their pricing structure?

Remember, your name will be associated with this referral, so treat it with the same care as you would if you were hiring them. Our word and referrals to our clients are very important.

Having this network is also a great way to stay connected with your clients after a transaction. I often remind my clients to reach out anytime they need a referral for ANYTHING.

Hairdresser, interior designer, party planner. . .I meet many different people in various industries. And the more I'm able to stay top of mind with my own client base and be a resource for them, the higher the likelihood they will remember me when someone else is asking for a referral for an agent.

MAINTAINING YOUR HEALTH AND SANITY

When asked why most people want to get into real estate (or be self-employed for that matter) the responses are:

1. Be my own boss
2. Flexible work schedule
3. Unlimited earning potential

This topic is quite subjective. Depending on your long-term goals, how efficient you are in your day, and your philosophy, the following may or may not be of interest to you, and all the above may or may not be possible for you. Here are some things I have found that have helped me maintain my sanity during this self-employed journey:

1. Working out. I found (despite trying hard to keep a schedule) that sometimes things happen, and my day can easily shift around. By working out in the morning, I was kick-starting my day in the right way, in an energized way and, regardless of what happened the rest of the day, my workout was complete. I was also less stressed about trying "fit it in" if things did go

all crazy. We all know the benefits of working out. So I'm not going to dive into that. I will say that from an energy and mental sanity perspective, working out has given me much more clarity, and feeling strong plays a big role in wanting and being able to accomplish more.

2. Take time to recharge. Take one day a week (at a minimum), take a proper lunch break (even if it's only twenty minutes to half an hour), book your vacation time. TAKE vacation time. It might seem like the harder you work, the more you will accomplish; however, your brain needs a break. *You* need a break. Operating at 60 percent for a long period of time doesn't serve anyone well. Not to mention that during these times, I started to resent what I was doing, which is also beneficial to no one. Taking the time to recharge to 90–95 percent will allow you to accomplish more in less time. AND: they say people accomplish WAY more the week before vacation because they know they are taking time off. What better way to give yourself a little push a few times a year?

3. If you are not good at setting time aside for yourself, book it in your calendar. They say you can tell a lot about what kind of year a person is going to have based on their calendar.

4. Put the good stuff in to get the good stuff out. I've heard MANY successful business people say that their mental health is much better served by tuning out (or turning off) the negative (the news) and spending the time instead by listening to or reading things of value—things that will actually improve your life, your mindset, your health, your overall well-being. It's amazing what happens when you actually stop listening to the news, and then you hear it one day. Try it—it's a very interesting experiment.

5. Eat well. Again—not a new topic. Being on the road a lot or working long hours, it's easy, for many, to eat what's available or perceived healthy versus what's actually good. Not all salads are healthy; not all "fresh" food is healthy. There are many options these days to have "ready-to-go" food.

a. Food delivery services: They deliver what you need to make a health(ier) meal. You are responsible for doing all the preparation.

b. Prepared food delivery food services: Meals that are already made and packaged into individual portion sizes are delivered to your door. Sometimes these can be frozen (so you can keep them in your freezer and use them when necessary) or if you prefer fresh, they are delivered mid-evening for the next day. They are easy to take along in the car (they often come delivered in a cooler bag), so you can grab and go. There are different companies, depending on your budget and food preferences (Vegan, Paleo, calorie specific, etc.). These can also be great for couples on the go or for some family nights when you know you won't have time to prepare a meal.

6. Your mindset and attitude play a big role in being self-employed. In fact, they can help control how you respond to very stressful situations, to clients and the possible hardships they will be experiencing (let's face it: real estate: both the transaction of real estate and the circumstances around why people might be buying and selling are emotional), and the ups and downs of running a business. Mindset has been proven to help with cognitive processing, problem-solving, decision-making, leadership (a skill required if you plan to have a team or people working for you and with guiding clients), and generally working with others. One thing I have become vividly aware of in real estate is all the different personality types that I work with—clients, service providers, or the different professionals I have hired for various work tasks.

This became extremely clear in my dealings with one of my website developers. We spoke two completely different languages. I mean not literally: he and I both spoke English, but how I was relaying ideas was not the way that he liked to receive information and nor was it in a way his mind processed things versus how my practical (slightly less descriptive) mind did. I didn't know the questions I needed to ask him to fully understand how I should be sharing my vision for the website. Nor did I ask him the best way to share my visions. After I received a mock-up that was NOTHING like I THOUGHT I had described, I learned some valuable (and expensive) lessons from this.

a) Face-to-face helps (although sometimes their preference is not to meet).

b) Drawings/diagrams/flowcharts—ALL are helpful.

c) Be clear about your goals and know how you want your client's experience to be. Depending on the developer, they might be able to share trends/ideas, but you are the salesperson and need to keep in mind your end goal.

Working on your mindset and attitude can have a direct correlation to the success of your business and your client (or even ALL your) relationships.

There are thousands of podcasts and books on the topic if you would like to explore it more. Either you are just starting or have dabbled in the concept before. The work can be quite extensive if you would like it to be.

One book that I found did a great job introducing the concept but also providing some other great life tips was *The 5 AM Club: Own Your Morning. Elevate Your Life* by Robin Sharma.

Working with someone you know versus someone you don't (when looking for a service provider)

This topic kind of falls under "how to keep your sanity" as well as who you should work with.

This will likely be a paragraph more on my experience versus "the facts," but sometimes experience is just as important.

Real estate can be very much a referral-based business. Most of us, when starting out, rely on the connections of our close friends and relatives. Being self-employed, I've often found myself in the position of wanting to help other self-employed people and/or other self-employed people who are also starting out, because I appreciated that others took the chance on me when I was new and isn't it just good karma? (It's possible I was naive there . . .)

This has worked out well for me in some instances and not so well in other instances.

Example: When I first started out, I needed help in designing my marketing materials. I was new to the whole concept of having to source a graphic designer (and back then, programs like Fiverr didn't exist). I asked around for graphic designer referrals. I was referred to a friend of a friend. She worked full time for a graphic design company and freelanced on the side. I thought this would be ideal: she was super experienced, a mutual connection, and because she was doing this through her own freelance company, the price would be more affordable for me.

It WAS more affordable—although it also never really got done. I spent three months waiting (past the articulated deadline), sending emails that were never followed up on, revisions never got completed, and finally, I was just worn out. It also made it very hard for me to see her around in social settings,- as the big elephant in the room was, "You still owe me materials that I paid for . . ."

Not all situations will end like this. Especially if you are mindful to ask some of the following questions:

1. Is this their full-time job or part-time job? If part-time, how will they manage the workload?
2. What is the cost structure? Sometimes it's better to pay more to have the job performed in a timely manner.
3. Speak to references. How has this person managed past jobs? Did they adhere to timelines?
4. How good have they been in communicating with you? Is there a long delay in response time?

5. How can you pay them? Do they only accept cash? Credit card? Will they be providing you an invoice for your expense?
6. Do you feel they will be respectful to the relationship you currently have with them?

Each situation is definitely going to be unique. And only you will be able to decide if you would prefer to work with someone you know versus a company where you might have more control over the outcome. Try both out and see what feels more comfortable to you.

One thing I will say: If you want to build your own business by referral and work with people that are CLOSE to you or your friends (who might be wary or afraid of working with you for fear it would jeopardize the relationship), make sure you do an outstanding job. Go over and above; give them ZERO opportunity to ever doubt or question passing your name along. If you take anything away from this book, it is this—be very, very respectful and appreciative for any and all referrals, and treat them like gold.

BE A PROFESSIONAL

I'm not sure if real estate is the only industry where the word "professional" is thrown around as frequently or as lightly as it is, but holy cow! The number of times I've been in a deal situation, and the other agent has opened up their "negotiation" with "I'm a PROFESSIONAL." It automatically sets off alarm bells for me. If you truly are something—I'm not sure there is a need to so openly (and without solicitation) declare it. But that's just my opinion.

Even though we have a regulatory board that outlines what "professional" should be, the actions can be quite different. Here are a few examples. I've had agents swear at me, hang up on me, take a phone call while otherwise occupied (aka: on the toilet and then flush), I've seen agents steal and lie to their benefit. I've seen them "challenge" our code of ethics because "why not see what really happens?"

When you are new, you might be more vulnerable to agents and clients playing on your lack of industry experience. You might find yourself in a position to do something that doesn't make you feel good, like cutting commission, lack of communication with co-operating agents, or just bending the system a bit because it could help you get your first deal. Remember: what you start doing will likely carry out for your career and, in some instances, could become habits (or bad habits) which could cost you your license.

Be respectful to everyone—regardless of who they are. We are blessed that we get to interact with so many different people in a day: office staff, neighbours, contractors, baristas, parking attendants, clients that are sad, clients that are happy, other agents. Being nice and mindful in the words and communication you choose can go a long way.

Karma is real. And for non-karma people, your reputation will always precede you. Or haunt you. Stay away from shady dealings; if it doesn't feel right, it probably isn't. If someone else is going to play dirty, maybe that's not your sandbox. There are plenty of wonderful agents who do care about the work they do for their client and how they treat their colleagues and can do it with integrity. However, I suspect if you are reading this, you are already one of them.

READING LIST

I've read many books over the course of being employed. Below are some that I have referenced in the various chapters or ones that I just felt are good reads if you would like to learn more about a specific topic.

Burchard, Brendon. *High Performance Habits: How Extraordinary People Become That Way*
Buffini, Brian and Niego, Joe. *Work by Referral*
Chilton, David. *The Wealthy Barber*
Chilton, David. *The Wealthy Barber Returns*
Elrod, Hal and Kiyosaki, Robert. *The Miracle Morning: The Not-So-Obvious Secret Guaranteed to Transform Your Life (Before 8 AM)*
Gladwell, Malcolm. *The Tipping Point*
Glason, George S. *The Richest Man in Babylon*
Grout, Pam. *E-Squared*
Hardy, Darren. *The Compound Effect*
Helmstetter, Shad. *What to Say When You Talk to Yourself*
Hill, Napoleon. *Think and Grow Rich*
Howes, Lewis. *The Mask of Masculinity*
Loehr, Jim and Schwartz, Tony. *The Power of Full Engagement*
Manson, Mark. *The Subtle Art of Not Giving a Fuck*
Pritchett, Price. *You2*

Serhant, Ryan. *Sell It like Serhant*

Sharma, Robin. *The 5 AM Club: Own Your Morning. Elevate Your Life*

Sincero, Jen. *You are a Badass*

Sincero, Jen. *You are a Badass at Making Money*

Sinek, Simon. *Start with Why*

Tracy, Brian. *Eat That Frog*

Voss, Chris. *Never Split the Difference*

THANK YOU

Thank you so much for purchasing this book. I am truly thankful. If you would like help with any of these sections please reach out.

www.jdconsult.ca

or

jendumitrescu3

I have various programs available to help—whether you are a new agent looking to get started, or an experienced agent that is looking to create systems and processes or looking to overhaul all the logistics that happen behind the scenes of your business so that you have more time to focus on what you do best and what you want to do.